Santa Fe Different

22 Years and All I Got Was a Cheeseburger

The ¡Órale! Columns

Arnold Vigil

Foreword by Max Evans

Museum of New Mexico Press
Santa Fe

Director: Anna Gallegos
Editorial director: Lisa Pacheco
Art director and book designer: David Skolkin
Composition: Set in Palatino with Silentia and Courier display
Manufactured in U.S.A.
10 9 8 7 6 5 4 3 2 1

Library of Congress Control Number: 2019953886

ISBN 978-0-89013-650-8 (paperbound)
ISBN 978-0-89013-651-5 (ebook)

Museum of New Mexico Press
PO Box 2087
Santa Fe, New Mexico 87504
mnmpress.org

Cover: Photograph by LeRoy N. Sanchez

Contents

Foreword

Reading *Santa Fe Different* reminded me how much I enjoyed Arnold Vigil's earlier work, especially *Forever New Mexico, Enduring Cowboys: Life in the New Mexico Saddle,* and *Backtracks: Time Travels through New Mexico.* In his columns and articles for the *Journal North,* the *Santa Fe New Mexican,* and *New Mexico Magazine* among other periodicals, he has uniquely captured the essence of the City Different, as it is historically and fondly called today, as well as New Mexico in general, with its majestic Sangre de Cristo Mountains, the Río Grande Gorge, patches of sagebrush desert, and sunsets in the high desert air, with colors that would have made the French impressionists jealous!

The columns collected in *Santa Fe Different* reveal his knowledge of a fabled city, his subtle sense of humor, and his rich understanding of what makes this world-renowned art center a comfortable home and destination for all.

¡Órale, Arnold! And muchas gracias!

—Max Evans
Author of *The Rounders, The Hi-Lo Country, Bluefeather Fellini, Madam Millie,* and too many others to list here

ÓRALE:
An Introduction

Órale: all right; OK, fine; Hi! Listen!
— Rubén Cobos, *A Dictionary of New Mexico and Southern Colorado Spanish*

For more than four years, from the fall of 2004 through 2008, I wrote a column called "¡Órale! Santa Fe" for the *Albuquerque Journal*'s northern bureau, also known as *Journal North*. This book is a select compilation of these columns, which appeared every two weeks in the newspaper.

I always heard about surprising things dropping into people's laps out of the clear blue sky; nothing of that sort had ever happened to me, except, perhaps, for that one dastardly citation for a traffic-light violation I received in the mail from the City of Albuquerque's unpopular and now defunct red-light-camera program. Then one day in 2004, out of nowhere, I received a call at my day job as an editor for *New Mexico Magazine* from Mark Oswald, the editor of *Journal North*, who asked me if I'd be interested in writing a column about Santa Fe. And here's the kicker: he said I could write about anything I wanted. Talk about the coyote dog-sitting the poodles!

Of course, I quickly learned that I was sloppy seconds, second fiddle, the bridesmaid and not the bride, numero dos, the rice and beans and not the enchilada. Oswald informed me that my former boss Larry Calloway, who was the editor of *Journal North* many, many moons ago when he hired me there as a police and courts reporter, recommended me for the column-writing gig after he had turned it down. Calloway, who as a UPI reporter was taken hostage by armed Chicano gunmen while he covered the infamous Río Arriba County Courthouse Raid in 1967, also wrote an entertaining column for many years in *Journal North* called "Mountain Ear" and later another about state government that ran in the main *Albuquerque Journal* editions.

Oswald's unexpected offer was exciting and one that I quickly accepted. But then the daunting time came around for the first column, then the second, then the third, and then the hundredth . . . talk about pressure to produce something fresh—even during the winter! But luckily, as a kid I paid attention to my mother, Margaret, chuckling while she read the newspaper and I became aware of some of the colorful writers who dutifully supplied columns to the *Santa Fe New Mexican* and other local publications. I drew inspiration from memories of their witticisms and insight. The earliest I can remember was a column in the early 1970s called "Los Bilingos" by Mary Ann Romero, whose daughter Carla was my elementary school classmate at E. J. Martínez School and then Harrington Junior High School. Carla sometimes was sheepish when the column came up in conversation because she and her siblings' daily lives were often the *chiste*, or the subject matter, for her mother's column.

As the years passed, I drew inspiration from other folksy writers who followed suit: Peter Eichstaedt and his "Adobe Joe" columns, the local witticisms of Orlando Romero in the *Santa Fe New Mexican*, the insightful writings and poems about northern New Mexico by the late Jim Sagel, who often wrote for *Journal North*, and, of course, our revered nationally famous New Mexican storytellers such as John Nichols, Rudolfo Anaya, and Max Evans. I first got to know Max Evans while downing beer and whiskey at an old bar on the old Mesilla Plaza after a premier of the digitally remastered movie *Lonely are the Brave*, filmed in 1962 around Albuquerque and starring Kirk Douglas, Walter Matthau, Gena Rowlands, Carroll O'Connor, and George Kennedy. The movie is based on the book *The Brave Cowboy*, written by Evans's departed friend Edward Abbey.

"Arnold, I can't watch this goddamned movie again! I've already seen it a hunnerd times," Max leaned over and told me just minutes before the flick was about to start at the newly renovated Fountain Theater. "Let's go have a drink at that bar on the plaza!"

"But Max, I've never seen this movie before and I want to see it!" I told him with much disappointment. "But I'll meet you there later." And boy oh boy did we meet up later, at least what I can remember of it!

Before meeting Max in person for the first time that night, I had had the honor of talking to him many times on the phone about feature stories and excerpts he previously wrote on assignment for *New Mexico Magazine*. His down-home writing style immediately captured me with passages like the time he described an outhouse: "It was a three-holer!" Or the time he described a dead animal he encountered while working on a ranch: "It broke my goddamned heart!" Luckily, he still remembered me some twenty years later when I dropped out of the clear blue sky and asked him to write a foreword to this book.

"¡Órale! Santa Fe" came to a sudden end during the economic downturn of 2008 when Mervyn's department stores stiffed the cash-strapped *Albuquerque Journal* reportedly to the tune of a million-dollar advertising debt. The newspaper first let go of freelance writers like me before they got rid of full-time positions and entire sections. "At least that's what they told me" is what I often told people at the time—but it turned out to be true; a whole slew of other popular writers and their columns were never to be seen or heard from again in the *Journal*. Although many of the other columnists wrote a final piece bidding fair thee well, explaining the situation, I never did give details to the loyal readers of "¡Órale! Santa Fe." I'm sure many of them thought my brain might have dried up or something. Or maybe they thought the *Albuquerque Journal* had had enough and decided to pull the plug on their little experiment to publish cheesy columns replete with occasional double entendres and Spanish cuss words that slipped through the cracks of the English-only-speaking editors—at least at first!

One such reader, my Aunt Angie in Albuquerque, was so disappointed that I no longer wrote the column that she pleaded with me to continue writing them on my own and sending them to her so that I "could keep in practice." Hmmm. I thought about that, and I wondered if plumbers or electricians or lawyers or even woodcutters continued their trades for free to keep on top of their game when there was no money to pay them for their skills. Actually, it made sense for a writer to do it and compile a stack of work should the opportunity of a column ever present itself again. But as any backhoe-drivin', TV-watchin', beer-drinkin' couch potato like me will admit, I'm only getting off my duff for another beer and more chips and, oh yeah, if nature calls. Besides, isn't there already a glut of unemployed writers out there who have joined the ranks of all the unemployed comedians who ply their unsolicited malarkey on the innocent passerby?

Therefore, herein, I have compiled a stack of battle-tested, mostly time-proof columns for those who might want to experience a loco local's view of Santa Fe as a change from the pretentiousness of the city usually presented in the high-society publications. The columns represent about half of those published in the *Journal North* and some have been updated (that's a fancy word writers use for "run through the wringer") to reflect time and circumstance while taking into account the all-too-familiar omnipresent factor: liability! People not intimately familiar with the storied past of New Mexico's capital city usually don't realize that there is an established local community with centuries-old lineage in this world-renowned town that now seems to be famous for being famous. All of us locals, who are trapped in the middle of this worldwide whirlwind of City Different popularity and have witnessed the abrupt changes in the city where we grew up, have varying opinions on the subject.

But sometimes, such an entrenched, intimate vantage does not have to be bitter or sad or critical or zealously approving for that matter. Sometimes it can be downright entertaining, depending on how you look at it. Some of the old column's readers have called me a chronicler; some ask if I'm still writing cartoons, while others ask if I still hate Chinese (Siberian) elms. All are fair comments and questions, and much more appreciated than those inquiring if I'm gaining weight and losing my hair!

Gold, Conquistadors, Cheeseburgers & Pizza

It could be argued that very little has changed in Santa Fe between the publication of this book and the last "¡Órale! Santa Fe" column, which appeared December 2008 in the *Journal North*. The plaza is still there and it is still mostly blocked. There are still downtown pedestrians galore, both locals and visitors, and many of them, like clockwork, walk in front of moving cars, a phenomenon now common in other places of town—especially with the onset of certain medical cannabis dispensaries where the patrons also park their cars and exit with the same indifference to traffic as hurried parents picking up their precious cargo after school lets out. And speaking of cannabis, the governor of Colorado recently boasted that Pueblo chile is superior to that grown in Hatch, sparking a very, very spicy debate. But I'm going to have to agree with the Colorado governor on that one because chile grown on the pueblos of Nambé, Pojoaque, San Ildefonso, and Ohkay Owingeh ranks right up there with Chimayó chile, the undisputed flavor champion! The governor to the north should realize that too many cooks ruin the chile stew and he should just stick with Mary Jane, you know, like "you dance with who brung ya!"

In addition to the heavenly smell of roasting chile that wafts through the crisp autumn air all over town, nature lovers are still able to feast their eyes upon the brilliant golden colors of changing aspens on the Sangre de Cristo mountainsides if the caterpillars haven't feasted on their leaves first. And local motorists still line up to bum rush yellow lights, which causes drivers going the other way to see red, and we all instinctively opt to avoid Cerrillos Road even though it's now one of the most efficient roadways for traffic flow this side of the Santa Fe River.

But there are some things that are different, such as the date Zozobra is burned. Now it's about a week before the start of La Fiesta de Santa Fe to be exact, and there's even an exclusive section to watch him burn right there front and center—for a hefty price! Nope, you can't bum rush that section any more no matter how early or late you show up. They used to torch Old Man Gloom a day before fiesta and it was popularly and incorrectly known as the official start of the centuries-old celebration. No more! (At least for the time being . . . the day has been changed so many times, it's becoming as unpredictable as the weather or, perhaps, the exact time of night when the giant white fella actually gets lit up!)

Even the ceremonial start to fiesta has changed, the most notable difference being the controversial Entrada pageant, which depicted Spanish soldiers peacefully and religiously retaking Santa Fe from the Indians more than a decade after the Pueblo Revolt. After several years of highly publicized and organized protests, the Entrada was removed from the fiesta's opening on the plaza gazebo that first Friday afternoon because of highly visible protests that it was not only insensitive to Pueblo culture but also historically inaccurate.

Now I admit that I always had a problem with the Entrada's boast that the reconquest of New Mexico was peaceful, and even more so when I learned about its likely beginnings. In Santa Fe native Charles Montgomery's carefully researched book *The Spanish Redemption*, the pageant was more than likely conceived by non-Native and non-Hispanic writers in the early 1900s as part of an overall tourism campaign to liven up and attract more visitors to La Fiesta de Santa Fe. The city fathers of the time felt that fiesta was too somber and religious and it needed more pizzazz to make it more interesting to visitors. (Sound familiar?)

During these fledgling years of the new and improved fiesta, local Anglo citizens donned historical garb to portray all the ethnic characters in the fiesta court that we know today. Of course, it didn't take too long before the critics at the time protested that the only things of color in the fiesta court were the lively costumes—including those portraying the Pueblo Indians, which featured feathered headdresses more representative of the Plains Indian tribes. Eventually, the cultural makeup of the fiesta court evolved to strictly represent who they were supposed to represent . . . the Spanish and the Pueblo Indians. So you could say, the Entrada was born of cultural protest and demised about a century later in cultural protest. Yep, you could call it about a hundred years of fake news! As of this writing, there have been no announcements or plans to rewrite the Entrada to more accurately depict actual history or to eliminate it forever.

The issue created quite the dilemma: How do we start the fiesta in Santa Fe—sans Entrada—with sympathetic modern PC values mixed with accurate historical facts, all with an entertaining flair to keep the tourists happy? Now if they had asked me, I would have suggested getting Willie Nelson and Waylon Jennings impersonators (and there are plenty of salty buskers nearby on the plaza who would gladly volunteer) to get up on the plaza gazebo and sing a tune to the melody of the duo's classic song "Mommas, Don't Let Your Babies Grow Up to Be Cowboys." Yep, I think with the contemporary mood of all things *entrada*-like, the song could go something like this:

Mammas, don't let yer babies grow up to be con-qui-sta-dors,
Don't let 'em wear armor 'n' go out searching for gold,
Make 'em stay home 'n' do as they're told.

Mammas, don't let yer babies grow up to be con-qui-sta-dors,
They'll just go out a wanderin' and a conquerin' new lands,
And four centuries later, they'll have so few fans.

So I guess there has been some degree of change in the City Different during the teenybopper years of the new millennium. But one thing definitely hasn't changed: it's still been fairly dry overall on the precipitation front. Although the reality of drought is ever so present, there was a very rare occurrence one night in the summer of 2018 when Santa Fe and its immediate surroundings suffered what was deemed the "thousand-year flood." That memorable storm dumped three inches of rain (sometimes about a year's worth in these parts) in about an hour and it wreaked havoc for those among us with leaky roofs and poor property drainage, not to mention the perennially dry arroyo banks.

But, personally, that thousand-year flood trickled in comparison with the horrible Susanami that upended my existence on the Black Tuesday of September 2011. That's when the then governor's crony state tourism cabinet secretary went office to office and informed me and many of my coworkers that our services were no longer needed at the Tourism Department and *New Mexico Magazine*, where most of us had worked as classified employees free of political interference for at least my nearly twenty-three years there. A so-called classified employee is supposed to have employment protections under state law, but we who were forced to walk the plank never figured out how the fine print on that one was interpreted by the Martínez administration.

And just like the fine print on a homeowner's insurance policy that won't cover catastrophic water damage due to acts of God, the mysterious fine print on our classified employment policy must have stated that we weren't covered by catastrophic damages caused by a Susanami . . . or acts by someone who thinks they're God.

Having endured many governor transitions during my state-employee career, five to be exact, I used to point out that every four years the

Americans would come and liberate us (classified employees). And toward the end of each administration the highly paid exempt employees (who were usually supervisors so that there would be "accountability") would start to drop like flies at the window on a blistering hot summer day. You could literally pull up a chair and watch the show, seeing them scramble for friends amongst those they had treated with condescension for years, while desperately looking for respite from the rising political heat. Another longtime classified veteran once shared this observation of the roulette wheel of old to new exempt employees: "The only thing that changes is the sound of the voices."

Well, in my case the Susanami came without warning in the form of a smiley-faced, golden-haired whippersnapper from the Pepsico corporate world of Chicago who was closely connected with some of the founding fathers of Taos Ski Valley, a favorite spot of mine. What a downhill blow!!! Anyway, as she went down the hall delivering unexplained pink slips to startled employees just after the lunch hour on that dastardly Black Tuesday, she suddenly appeared at my door accompanied by an obviously distressed and uncomfortable state personnel officer. The darling of the Susanami world quickly informed me with little explanation that I was to vacate my office of more than twenty-two years by closing time—and that was no small order with more than two decades of accumulated but useful editorial crap scattered randomly throughout the premises but precisely where someone in the know could locate it.

Then she reached out to shake my hand, flashing her top and bottom chompers and almost as if bouncing on her toes, perkily told me, "Thank you for your service to the State of New Mexico." WHAM!!! All I could think of as a response was, "I should at least get a ski pass out of this!"

"Well, I can't get you a ski pass, but I can get you a cheeseburger," she replied with a signature grin that had a knack for charming the unsuspecting before the ensuing lethal bite. I can only remember that scenario now as my own personal "Here's Johnny!" moment like that from Jack Nicholson's movie *The Shining*, based on the book by suspense/thriller-champion Stephen King.

So, my friends, I enthusiastically promoted my cherished state for almost twenty-three years, not as a Democrat or a Republican but as a proud New Mexican . . . for a cheeseburger! Gee thanks! And for those who are wondering, I wasn't going to shake that hand until after it handed over my cheeseburger, complete with green chile, extra onions, and double meat to boot! I've long since given up on the wait!

"Let them eat cake," an infamous Marie once said. And in my case, the lethally blonde must have thought, "Let them eat cheeseburgers" in classic New Mexico True, green-chile form. Turns out, this golden girl did such a fantastic job introducing the cold, indifferent corporate world to New Mexico tourism that the Susanami cast her away to lead the troubled state CYFD, known more precisely as the Children, Youth and Families Department, left in shambles by the last exempt cabinet secretary.

The Susanami inevitably washed itself up after leaving this state in the doldrums and, thankfully, stopped ruining so many innocent lives in its mostly negative path. And, ironically, it wasn't the shallow promises of cheeseburgers, or skipping out on paying for them either, that ultimately helped bring an end to its vindictive and mostly unnecessary devastation. It was peeetza!

Now that's something to chew on!

—Arnold Vigil

Part 1
Cerrillos Road

Some folks who arrived here long before me remember life before the bulldozers came and knocked down whole sections of established neighborhoods to make way for the thoroughfares that would become St. Francis Drive, Guadalupe Street, and Paseo de Peralta.

It's Not Called the City Different for Nothin'

Back in my youth, a lot more people used to refer to Santa Fe as the Ancient City. Today, nearly a handful of businesses listed in the phone book use the words "ancient city" in their title.

Technically, Santa Fe doesn't qualify to be accurately classified as ancient, but that doesn't stop some of us from calling it that, or naming our town after any other antiquated aspect of the city that has ingrained itself so intensely into our hearts. For almost a century we've also adoringly called our community the City Different. Although some have passionately objected to the moniker, I believe for locals, or anybody else who's lived here for any period of time no matter how long, that name is quite appropriate in more ways than one.

Ask anyone who genuinely cares about this city and they'll probably recall the first time they became attached to one of Santa Fe's endearing characteristics and then they'll voice their dismay when they realized it became "different." In fact, you'll notice how emotionally "different" they become from when they first start telling their story to when they finish—if they do manage to finish, because, as we all know, this is an ongoing saga.

For some, it might be the time they first noticed a trophy house appearing on the dying piñon-and-juniper-studded hills east of the city and how it interrupted the natural order of the tree line that had existed there for centuries. The first ridgetop home I can remember popped up on a hill just north of upper Cerro Gordo Road in the early 1980s, and it was quite visible from nearly anywhere in the city, especially at Canyon Road Park, er, I mean Patrick Smith Park. Soon thereafter, many others followed and today the peppering of large homes across hills all around the city is all too common.

I like to compare this Santa Fe hill-peppering phenomenon to the first nick or dent you get on a brand-new car. Boy, that first one hurts the most! But after a few trips to the mall or to the office or wherever else cars are prone to congregate, you soon notice your car door is splattered with multicolored nicks and tiny dents. But all the new nicks don't seem to bother you as much after that first one. You just accept it as inevitable.

Today, after decades of hillside construction in both the city and the county, any time a new fabulous home goes up, many of us hardly seem to notice. Apparently the only ones who do notice are the nearby neighbors, who probably fought tooth and nail to prevent it, just as the activists did when their own home went up. But these dream homes aren't popping up as frequently as they used to because of a variety of "different" reasons, including the ever-changing political face of our local governing bodies, the roller-coaster economy, and the severity of recent drought conditions that is limiting growth.

The successive dry seasons we've had throughout the past decade, coupled with the explosion of the bark beetles, have killed off most of our once plentiful piñon trees. Nowadays when you look up to the hills, all you're likely to see are juniper trees, piñon-tree carcasses, and trophy homes, most of which have already been cleared of the dead piñons within their property boundaries.

Because of this, I, as a writer, can no longer honestly use that cliché many writers love to use when describing our city's environs: the "piñon-and-juniper-studded hills." Maybe from now on, in the spirit of being accurate, I should only refer to them as our "juniper-and-rico-studded hills." Don't get me wrong, though—I lost those unscathed hill views a long time ago and I've had a lot of time to get over my sadness about how they look now. In fact, if I ever win the lottery, them juniper-and-rico-studded hills are the first place I'm gonna look for a new home. (Then I can write about how marvelous it is to live there and how mistaken I was before my good fortune.) I just hope that when I move up there, I don't drive the property values down too much. With newly won lottery riches, I'd much rather move my family to the foothills overlooking Santa Fe than to some gaudy mansion in smoggy California where we'd become the Beverly Vigilbillies.

Smashing back down to earth, however, there are many more varieties of moments when local people realized their hometown had become the City Different since they grew up. Some folks who arrived here long before me remember life before the bulldozers came and knocked down whole sections of established neighborhoods to make way for the thoroughfares that would become St. Francis Drive, Guadalupe Street, and Paseo de Peralta. It's hard to imagine life here now without these crucial arteries, or the simple life before when far-fetched ideas such as handling massive traffic flow existed only in the minds of the doomsayers. I can imagine seeing the sadness in these same people's eyes when they actually realized that most of their own hard-working children would not be able to afford a humble home in the same neighborhood where so many of their family's forebears had once lived.

But before I get too teary-eyed thinking about this, I often remind myself of former mayor Sam Pick's words when he succinctly commented about the locals' loss of ancestral habitat: "Nobody held a gun to their head to make them sell." I remember that when I first read his quote in the newspaper, my first reaction was to be up in arms. But before the short time my arms reached their full stretch to the ceiling,

I knew he was right. My eldest sister often put it this way: When locals sell, "it's either for need or greed" (and I didn't even know she was a poet).

People in my generational curve knew Santa Fe had become the City Different when we could no longer cruise the plaza in its entirety. Okay, I admit it. I'm not ashamed to say that I have cruised and still enjoy cruising the plaza, even though it's now only about half the fun it used to be. Cruising the plaza is one of the few reasons I have left to go downtown any more, and I prefer to skirt by in my car because I'm terrible on a skateboard (and at dodging them, too).

Even if I do win the lottery, I'm sure I'll still avoid shopping downtown and I'll do most of my bargain hunting down Cerrillos Road way or on St. Michael's Drive or Rodeo Road. But you can bet the ranch that I'll still be cruisin' the plaza on the way back to my home in the juniper-and-rico studded hills—Walmart bags and all!

Things We'll Never See Again

You can pretty much bank on certain things never happening again in this world. Don't believe that ancient law of physics that says what goes up must come down, because the price of gas is transforming that wise old man's saying into an old wives' tale. We'll probably never see gas dip below $2 a gallon again, just as we'll never see Janet Jackson perform in another Super Bowl halftime show.

We'll never again see time come to a standstill so that families and friends can huddle together around a radio to listen to the heavyweight championship of the world "live and for free," just as we'll never again be able to waltz through an airport totally uninterrupted to board a plane. We'll never again be able to jump on a horse and ride from one county to another without hopping a fence, crossing a busy highway, or trespassing on someone's land, just as we'll never be able to drive up to a liquor store after work and buy a six-pack of beer and a half-dozen tamales without getting out of the car.

Closer to home, it's probably a pretty safe bet that we'll never see another mobile home pop up anywhere east of St. Francis Drive, just as we'll never see another swish sail through the hoop at Sweeney Gymnasium. We'll never see another statue of Juan de Oñate (or any conquistador, for that matter) go up without a divisive community fight, just as we'll never see a rich and famous big shot cause a big stir for wanting to build his trophy home off Airport Road.

Yes, it's quite obvious that life in the past seemed to be a tad more laid back and easier than today. That's why sometimes it's hard to blame some of those in our community who spend a lot of time—and money—trying to keep our lives in the past, at least on the surface.

I'm sure that a pretty good number of my ancestors would have been quite shocked if they had ever known that the traditional adobe style of their time, which essentially evolved out of practicality and necessity through the centuries, heavily influenced the architectural style of choice of the ricos in our fair town, albeit on a much grander scale. Back in the days of the *ancianos*, adobe and mud plaster and doors, windows, and furniture handcrafted from local wood were the look and style of the peasants in the eyes of the newly arrived Easterners coming out west to exotic Santa Fe to seek adventure and fortune when New Mexico became a US territory after the Mexican War.

But soon after the turn of the twentieth century, a more philanthropic crowd began arriving on the stagecoaches and the trains, and they took a more sympathetic look at the native people and their simple earthen structures and agrarian lifestyles. They adopted both traits wholeheartedly and took steps to preserve them. Thus Santa Fe Style was born, a melding of Spanish Colonial, Pueblo, and Territorial cultures.

There's no doubt that an anciano, draped in his worn denim coveralls and scruffed-up work boots and puffing his hand-rolled *cigaro* with one hand while holding his favorite shovel with the other, would be quite surprised that the peasant style of his time had evolved into the rico style of today. I'm sure he'd also be surprised that his steady diet of chile, beans, posole, and tortillas, also the perceived symbols of the lower class during his time, had become popular staples craved by all classes in most of the local restaurants and homes.

No doubt if we could get the Starship Enterprise to beam him up from his era to today, he'd be more than ready to start making adobes and start constructing a home himself on the vacant field nobody in his family wanted because it was on a hill too far away from the Acequia Madre. He'd be ready to transform himself into a modern, upstanding rico Eastsider just by being himself.

I don't think I'd have the heart to tell him that first he would need a permit from the city to start building, but only after he had clear title to the land, which was being held up in court over a boundary dispute with the rico neighbor next door, who is contending that the old cottonwood stump never constituted a true property line and all prior surveys were null and void because nobody contested his ownership of his lot all the way to the road.

(Of course, we'd have Captain Kirk make good for our anciano and have him assign Spock to sort through all the sordid historical details of this rare and valuable piece of vacant Eastside land, including the family transfers, foreclosures, card games, contentious divorces, hazy in-law inheritances, flips and flops, the Santa Fe Ring, etc., etc., etc.)

And after the Enterprise made sure our anciano friend made it through all those obstacles and quieted the rico neighbor on that side, he'd still have to deal with the group of city-appointed, modern-day philanthropists who would sternly but somewhat kindly point out to him how he would have built the home in his day. At the hearing, they would inform him what color he would have painted his house trim, where he would have situated his windows, doors, and front wall, and what direction he would have put his driveway. And by the way, they would insist to our era-jumper that there's no way he would have put up a tin roof during such a dry period, even though the material was readily available down at Big Jo's. This down-to-earth, God-fearing man from the past would soon be forced to see the devil—in the details.

There is no doubt that our anciano visitor would also be heartbroken when this same group of well-meaning, historical-minded stylists told him that there's no way he could build a *cuartito* (toolshed) out of scrap lumber, even though the still usable material was a goodwill gesture from the *rica* neighbor on the other side who really just wanted it out of her yard because she didn't want to pay anybody to haul it to the dump.

And I'm sure this anciano time traveler, who is surely perplexed by now, will never figure out which rico neighbor curiously looked over from the road and then called the state engineer on him when he began digging holes first for his outhouse, then for his well, which he desperately needed to start making adobes for his Santa Fe Style home before his building permit expired.

No doubt it was this same nosy neighbor's large, loose, purebred dog that absconded with the bones from the dirt pile that later turned out to be ancient human remains, which then forced another delay of the whole project.

This master builder of the past surely was never hit with a red tag during his day, and I'm sure by now he's ready to jump into the well or at least what was to be the well—from a ladder. "Scotty, beam this anciano outta here! This history experiment has gone awry. He is not qualified for Santa Fe Style!"

Yep, there's yet another thing we'll surely never see again. We'll never again witness another Santa Fe Style home built in the same authentic style that spawned Santa Fe Style.

They Are the "Peelers" of the Community

Scientists from the National Institutes of Health discovered that by switching off a single gene that regulates dopamine, they were able to make laboratory monkeys work harder. Dopamine, they report, controls the brain's ability to sense when a payoff is due for a worked-for task.

In other words, these research scientists were able to make monkeys work like ants. With their dopamine receptors turned off, the animals didn't procrastinate and they worked vigorously and longer to achieve a goal with no anticipation of a reward.

This exciting scientific discovery caught my interest because, if applied to humans, it could mean the end of "peeling" as we know it. Now for those who don't know what peeling is all about, I'll supply you with a little background. Peeling is a northern New Mexico slang word equivalent to the mainstream terms of "loafing," "slacking off," "taking it easy," "kicking back," "the life of Riley."

In fact, if you're reading this (and you most definitely are), you're more than likely peeling it at this very moment! (Especially if your feet are propped up on the desk or on a table and you're procrastinating before taking on the next task at hand.)

Go to any construction site and there's a good chance the plumbers are calling the electricians a bunch of peelers, and the electricians are calling the roofers the peelers, and the roofers are calling the framers the peelers, and so on and so forth. Most of the time they're kidding, however, unless they're waiting on each other to finish so that they can get going with their own jobs (which is most of the time). About the only time these guys are on the same page is when they're all waiting on the city inspector, who's been known to be a few minutes, hours, or days late for an assessment. You can only guess what they're calling this fine public servant (in addition to peeler) while they wait.

There are some construction-oriented folks, however, who are actually legitimate peelers. They're the rough-looking fellows who supply all of the roofing vigas, which are usually large pine logs from the forest that have to be peeled (as in removal of their bark) for use. Now it's just not too smart to go up to one of these burly wood haulers and call him a peeler. More than likely he'll whack you upside the head with a *latilla*—and a peeled one at that.

I don't know exactly how this distinctly New Mexican piece of slang came into being. It's been around all my life and it could be a form of Spanglish. The interesting thing about the idea of "peeler" is that it can be applied to all walks of life, not just construction. The employees at the lab in Los Alamos have been known (on their coffee breaks, of course) to call the state employees in Santa Fe a bunch of peelers. And if there's any peeling going on up there on the Hill, well, we'll never know because that's "classified." It might all come out in a top-secret peeler investigation, if you know what I mean.

Public employees are easy targets for those peeling salvos hurled by the public. I'm sure many public servants have had a recurring nightmare of investigative reporter Larry Barker chasing them down the hall screaming, "Is it true you're a peeler? We have hidden-camera footage of you peeling it!"

On the other hand, a peeler's fantasy is having Larry Barker chase former investigative reporter Conroy Chino down the hall in the same fashion. After a successful career of chasing down a few peelers himself, Chino switched over to public service as state labor secretary for a short stint and then went back into the private sector. No chance of that now.

One time during one of my hard-earned vacations from my highly demanding day job, I had just finished a multiple-hour workout at the gym. When I was leaving, Randy, the spa manager, put down his newspaper, sat up in his chair, and barked out at me in front of a group of people, "Arnold, don't you ever work?!"

"Sure," I replied. "Don't you know how many hours I have to peel it to afford this place?"

I don't know if the word *peeler* will ever make it into mainstream America, but there's always a chance. I could just imagine presidential candidates calling their opponent a peeler. The other candidate would rebut by telling the American people that if they elected the other candidate, the country would be run by a bunch of peelers.

If the word went mainstream, western movies would show the town preacher hovering over the casket of the deceased town drunk, clutching his Bible with one hand and pointing a crooked finger at the sky with the other, declaring, "He was a peeler of the community!" Late-night television infomercials would ask, "Do you desire a high-paying, peel-it job? Then a career in management could be for you!"

Many people who know me ask the inevitable question "Why did you feel compelled to write about peeling it?" I tell them that in order to write well, you must write what you know. And I still don't know if my daytime boss at the time ever read this—with his feet propped up on the desk while at work!

If those scientists ever succeed in stopping all monkeys from being peelers, how would our primordial cousins ever peel their bananas? They'd starve. And how, God forbid, could they be monkeys if they could never monkey around? It's just not natural.

Someone needs to stop these hardworking scientists before they apply this to humans, because we all need our peelers of the community. If there were no more peelers, then what would we point at so that we could feel better about ourselves?

Walk to the Plaza

For years, I had seen the seemingly endless portraits of beautiful Santa Fe real estate agents upon page after page of homes for sale in this special hometown of mine. The first time I ever saved enough money to cover a down payment on a home, I routinely pored over these realty booklets and advertisements looking for the perfect place that would be the first major purchase of my life.

After I finished scanning over all the "simply mahvelous" faces and wondered which one of them would lead me to the best bang for my buck, I looked at the prices. Man, talk about sticker shock! The process of buying a home in Santa Fe was quite the eye-opener for a then free-spending whippersnapper such as myself. After I got over the ensuing feelings of inadequacy and low self-worth, if you know what I mean, I got down to the practicality of finding a home in my earning range.

I quickly learned to look for certain catch phrases in the home listings while I avoided others like the plague. For instance, every time I saw "walk to the plaza," I knew the humble abode in question was out of my league because of the pricey privilege of living near downtown. Besides, anytime I went to the plaza, with the downtown parking situation as it is, I ended up walking there anyway—from my faraway parking spot. In my college days, I used to rent an apartment near downtown and sometimes I would "walk to the plaza" for an evening of happy night-clubbing minus the worry of driving home. But after the hours of fun and frolic were over, I would "stagger home from the plaza." Somehow, I don't envision a real estate agent trying to sell a home near downtown by writing "crawl home from the plaza" or "walk a crooked line home from the plaza."

Realistically, in my price range, a more appropriate phrase for a house listing would be "walk to K-Mart." I don't anticipate seeing that one anytime soon—or others, either. Like "walk home from jail" or "walk to Cheeks." If children could buy homes, they would look for phrases like "walk to McDonald's" or "walk to the Children's Museum." I'm sure a real estate agent could make a home anywhere in town sound attractive to a faithful buyer by using the catchwords "walk to Chimayó," especially during Lent.

After thorough review, however, I realized the ads for affordable homes in my price range contained phrases like "fixer-upper" and "needs some TLC." For those homes, honest real estate agents should insert an additional passage such as "walk to Home Depot." And if the affordable home is for sale in a rough neighborhood, *TLC* could mean "todos locos Chicanos." On that same note, some of the gentrified neighborhoods on the Eastside could use "some TLC." The now ritzy neighborhoods used to have some locos chicanos in the olden days. They were called pachucos. To utter a phrase in the spirit of the late comedian George Carlin, "then the real estate values skyrocketed and the pachucos went away."

After a while, I started instinctively ignoring the beautiful faces (some complete with their beloved purebred pooches) and just compulsively looked for "TLC" and the usually accompanying low price. To me, *TLC* didn't stand for "tender loving care." It stood for "the local's cost" and if it required me having to learn how to use a left-handed screwdriver, then so be it.

Needless to say, the TLC approach didn't work out. Every place I looked at was in major need of the TLC of a similar but different ilk: "time, labor, collateral." I just didn't have the time for major construction. Luckily, about that same time my girlfriend (she later became my wife) offered to pool her resources with me to buy a house and we were able to up the ante a notch or two. No longer were elbow grease, a strong backbone, and a reliable pickup the major considerations in my quest for homeownership.

Still, a place east of St. Francis Drive was definitely out of the question. So we kept our eyes open for a listing like "mountain-bike to the plaza" or "less than a gallon of unleaded to the plaza." Finally, with the assistance of one of those mahvelous-looking, SUV-driving real estate agents, and after many cozy rides in his new gas guzzler, we found a place on the southwest side. After loan applications, closing costs, papers to sign, etc., we were finally homeowners. In the process, we also learned what the previous owner had paid for the house just a handful of years earlier. Boy, did that juicy information rain on our parade! But as life in real estate goes on, the tables were turned when we sold the house a decade later and the buyer inquisitively asked me what we had originally paid.

This introduction to the Santa Fe real estate market decades ago reminds me of the time a group of us spent a hundred bucks a ticket to watch Julio César Chávez box in Las Vegas, Nevada. We entered the MGM Grand arena and eagerly looked down toward the ring, wondering where we would sit. For a hundred bucks, our seats surely would be close to ringside. Not a chance. The usher pointed us up—not down—to our perches. During the rest of the fight card, we chuckled as we looked down at the others entering the arena who also anxiously looked toward the ring but then were directed upward. The surprised looks on their faces as they looked upward no doubt matched ours just moments before.

Admittedly, I felt a little better as I stood in a long line for a beer. The man behind me began complaining that he spent $1,500 a ticket to sit in the bleachers above the ringside seats. Here he had spent $1,400 more on a ticket than me and he still had to wait in that slow-moving line alongside the rest of us pikers to get drunk.

I guess that boxing analogy could sum up the human side of real estate in Santa Fe, or anywhere else for that matter. You think you paid too much when you made the purchase, but you complain that the value is not that high when the tax bill arrives. In the meantime, however, you feel better when someone moves into the neighborhood and the price they paid for a similar home a few years after your purchase was considerably more—and they still have to wait in that overcrowded intersection for three light changes at rush hour just like you do. And when it comes time to sell, well, all those prior passionate feelings go out the window because the value of your home, no matter what shape it's in, is never high enough!

Life has been good to many of those dabbling in Santa Fe real estate, and as long as human nature will be human nature, I expect the values of homes in all parts of town to keep climbing. There are enough of those human tendencies to go around on all sides. But boy do I ever feel sorry for some of our local youth who will want to buy their first home in the upcoming years. At this rate, it's getting farther and farther to walk to the plaza.

The Code of Santa Fe Can Be Useful

In the not-too-distant past, one of our esteemed county commissioners tried in vain to get his fellow commissioners to pass a motion to publish a version of the *Code of the West* specific to Santa Fe County. This code would have been available to help people pondering a move to rural Santa Fe or even folks already living there.

Now those of you who are more well-read than the rest of us know that the original *Code of the West* was a novel penned by the famed Western writer Zane Grey in the early 1900s. The story extolled the honorable virtues of the self-reliant people of the West and how they routinely helped their fellow human beings and always took the high road on all matters, etc., etc.

More recently, however, a man by the name of John Clarke, a commissioner for Larimer County, Colorado, created a modified version of the *Code of the West* that outlined many different aspects of life in the rural Western United States. The code basically explains what people should expect when they decide to relocate to a rural area that lacks the governmental amenities that urban areas enjoy, including emergency services, law-enforcement protection, adequate access to utilities, and well-maintained roads.

Clarke's *Code of the West* made such an impact that not only his county but other counties throughout Colorado, Arizona, and even as far north as Washington adopted specific versions of it as part of their official county policies.

Among some of the issues addressed in the code are access (emergency response, right of way, road maintenance, dust, delivery service); utilities (telephone, water, sanitation, laws governing well use and septic tanks); property (building codes, easements, land limitations, geological hazards, light codes, ditch access); mother nature (fire vulnerability, slope slides, soil density, drainage, wildlife danger, insects); and agriculture (smells, chemicals, livestock, noxious weeds).

CODE OF SANTA FE

Most of the material in Clarke's *Code of the West* is pretty useful stuff and I wondered why our own County Commission backed out of publishing a version of it for the Santa Fe area. Maybe there were too many idiosyncrasies in our neck of the woods that are clearly understood but better left unsaid for good public relations.

I also wondered if the job of authoring the *Code of Santa Fe* would have been left to local-government scribes or if a committee would have been appointed to develop the code. I recall one colorful rancher from Carlsbad (and a county commissioner at the time, come to think of it) who gave his take on government-appointed committees during an interview: "If a government committee was in charge of designing a bird, it would fly backwards," he quipped in his southern New Mexico drawl. Others say the camel is the result of a committee that designed a horse.

Well, if the idea is ever resurrected here for either the county or the city, I offer a small smattering of insights for both newcomers and long-entrenched locals to get the ball rolling on a new *Code of Santa Fe*.

Demographics: Santa Fe is known as the "City Different" because of its difference from other cities in the nation. But after living here for a while, you might be tempted to call it the "City Different Dimension." Why? Because a healthy percentage of our residents appear to live right here and now, but in their minds they believe Santa Fe has changed and they prefer to live in the Santa Fe that used to be.

Also, another steadily growing percentage of residents, apparently here and now, are actually living in a Santa Fe that they believe should become like somewhere else.

There is also a smaller percentage of people in Santa Fe that are, indeed, living in the here and now but are also living somewhat in the future. By the way, this percentage of residents will be more than happy to help you sell your home and/or help you find a new one.

Property: You now know that Santa Fe is called the "City Different," but after living here for a stretch, you might be tempted to call it the "City Differential." Why?

Because even a casual look at the real estate pages will reveal the difference in property values on the eastern fringes compared with the western fringes. And expect the prices asked for the lower-priced "affordable" sections on the west and south sides to well exceed average home prices in the rest of the state and a good part of the nation. In other words, it's expensive across the board to live here, so keeping up with the Joneses will put you to the task, especially on the Eastside, where there just might be a billionaire living behind that newly built wall and automated entry gate.

If you happen to relocate to a historic neighborhood, expect that first the neighbors, then city inspectors, will put more thought into your home-improvement project than you did. Abrupt courses in building codes are not uncommon, especially from brash fellow citizens who had their own previous home-improvement plans vetoed.

Personal Responsibility: Living in a historic Santa Fe structure also carries added responsibility, like promptly reporting to authorities the ancient human remains workers dug up in your backyard while they planted a water-guzzling tree, or underneath your bathroom when you decided to update your plumbing. Or, perhaps, as a matter of survival, forcing yourself to be cordial to the former occupants' questionable relatives or friends who will occasionally pay you an unexpected late-night visit from time to time.

Rankings: Much is said about New Mexico's and Santa Fe's low rankings nationwide in areas of education, government services, health care, and so forth. But rest assured we rank near the top in lewd comments shouted out of car windows at women on the street.

Such low rankings, however, do present a positive side. They provide plenty of scapegoats to blame instead of your own shortcomings.

Games of Chance: Gambling is legal at many nearby Indian casinos, but if taking chances at losing hard-earned money is not your cup of tea, there are other ways to play games of chance.

For instance, mail something important to a relative or friend from Santa Fe's US Post Office and take a chance that it will arrive there in time or even the current year. Or during inclement weather, place your garbage outside for pickup and take a chance that the hard-working city garbage crews will get to it before the neighborhood dogs.

Closely follow the third car into the congested intersection during a red light at rush hour and take a chance there's not a policeman somewhere within sight. But note, sometimes the cop's car is the second one in that line and, if that's the case, there is no third or fourth car through.

And the last game of chance: Write a cheesy column about the *Code of Santa Fe* and take a chance you're not making someone mad who will have to assist you with some type of necessary service in the future.

Farolito vs. Luminaria: One Hot Issue

One summer, a large group of my family and our friends got together in a beautiful northern New Mexico mountain location for our annual family reunion. Just about that time the Bush-Kerry presidential race was gaining steam and heading into the final stretch. Gauging from the conversation, most of my *gente* were in John Kerry's corner, and the choir was humming in harmony with the preacher for quite a long while.

It wasn't until one cousin in particular showed up with her husband from Albuquerque late one afternoon that things began to get more interesting. My cousin's husband had no qualms about being a staunch Republican, and he had made this quite clear to us *norteños* years ago when Gary Johnson was our esteemed governor, although he backed off a bit when Johnson zigzagged his supporters by coming out in favor of legalizing marijuana.

So it wasn't surprising that my cousin's husband was quite outspoken about his choice for president. He never beat around the Bush!

George Dubya was his man and he was not going to back down one bit. It didn't matter how many people were good-naturedly talking trash about his choice of candidate. He held his ground valiantly on that pine-covered hillside until, I think, he realized he was surrounded. There was no way this Duke City man was going to win this discussion, especially in northern New Mexico, so he stepped back and took a breath.

"Come on, guys, let's talk about something else," he interjected. "No one's going to win this argument—even though Bush is going to win the election."

He just couldn't resist getting in another zinger and the topic of politics lived on for another several rounds of ribbing and jocularity, only this time a few decibels higher, a bit more spirited, and maybe with a little more finger-pointing.

"No, really, you guys, let's talk about something more pleasant," he again pleaded to the group, which was drawing closer and closer around him. "Let's talk about luminarias and all the nice things we like to do for Christmas in New Mexico."

Everybody paused and looked at each other, all obviously tired of the heated exchanges and the discussion going nowhere, just like a cat chasing its tail. Luminarias seemed tame enough, so the conversation shifted gears.

"Luminarias are great," I told him. "Sometimes we like to roast marshmallows or even hot dogs on them for fun, especially when we're hungry."

"I bet that takes you a long time to roast that wienie over that little candle," he retorted, looking at me with that same shit-eating grin he had used before. "And don't you get sand all over it when you're trying to squeeze it into the bag?"

"What?!!!" I exclaimed. "You must be from Albuquerque, because over there they call *farolitos* luminarias. You guys all believe them pretty-boy anchormen on the news who can't say 'farolito' without butchering it, just like every other word in Spanish. They don't even try to pronounce it correctly."

"No, it's been scientifically proven that the little bags with candles are called luminarias," he blurted right back. "I just saw it on the news the other day. They came from China, you know?"

And before you know it, once more there was a crowd around this guy and the zingers again were piercing the slight warm breeze in the air. Only this time everybody was wigging out about farolitos and luminarias—and it wasn't even close to Christmas!

It was like a Chicano version of the "Tastes Great, Less Filling" exchanges in the old beer commercials.

By this time my cousin had come to her husband's rescue and she told him it was time to go help her make dinner. "Here, have a cigar," he told me, handing me a big fat stogie and obviously happy to be getting away from the contentious group. "I'll be smoking one of these on election night."

"Well, you better save one for Christmas," I yelled back at him. "Then you can light it by sticking your head into the luminaria. It might burn some sense into you."

"Don't worry, I'll be sure to get the candle out of the bag to light this puppy," he said, motioning toward his cigar.

Before I could politely correct him again, he and my cousin had already disappeared into the peace and comfort of their expansive fifth-wheel RV.

I didn't get a chance to ask him this question: If he calls the little bags *luminarias*, then what does he call the little bonfires? I was going to suggest that he call them *fire-litos*, as a matter of fairness, since he wasn't going to budge an inch on either luminarias or politics.

Now that we all know Bush won that election, I suggested at future family reunions we start out talking about religion and then, perhaps, move on to Dr. Spock's methods of raising children. If we're all still talking to each other after that, then we might be able to rekindle the subject of farolitos. It'll be our own little New Mexican version of the Mason-Dixon Line, the Hatfields vs. the McCoys, or exercise vs. liposuction.

Every holiday season, the luminaria-farolito issue comes front and center again.

For me, I know it's time to get into the spirit of Christmas when I hear the locals cursing at the television screen after hearing the news anchors calling the little candlelit bags luminarias, or when I'm stopped on the street by a friendly tourist who asks me in a Texas drawl, "We're staying at the El Diadora [Eldorado Hotel]. Can you tell me where we kin git a good look-see at dem bag-a-litas?"

Oh well, at least she came closer to "farolito" than my cousin's husband from Albuquerque.

The Quest for Commonality

Television, motion pictures, and professional sports traditionally have wielded a great influence on the average American, and many people talk about the responsibility of such media to provide positive role models for our youth.

It's probably hard for young people today to realize that just a few decades ago, there were very few highly recognizable Spanish-surnamed television and movie stars in the United States. And even some of these celebrities changed their names so that their Latino background was not quite so apparent.

Movie stars such as Anthony Quinn (Antonio Rodolfo Quinn Oaxaca) and Rita Hayworth (Margarita Carmen Cansino) came from Latino backgrounds, Mexican and Spanish, respectively, as did baseball legend Reggie Jackson, a Puerto Rican whose complete name is Reginald Martínez Jackson. Cesar Romero kept his Cuban surname and still made it big, but Raquel Welch did not keep her original last name—Tejada.

Today, Martin Sheen and Charlie Sheen took on different stage names from their backgrounds, but Charlie's brother, Emilio Estevez, did not.

Spanish-surnamed athletes are commonplace nowadays, especially in professional baseball, where many athletes have come to the United States from a whole slew of Latin American countries. There's even a smattering of Latino names who have broken into the elite ranks of professional football and basketball, as well as golf and tennis.

More recently, we've seen the *George Lopez Show*, as well as *Freddie*, starring Freddie Prinze Jr., who lived in Albuquerque and whose father, Freddie Prinze, was one of the first Hispanics to star in his own television show, *Chico and the Man*. There's even a character actor named Miguel Sandoval, who appears in many movies and television serials and who grew up right here in Santa Fe.

But back in my youth, there were very few names that appeared on television that reflected my own northern New Mexico Hispanic background. Sure there was Desi Arnaz, the memorable Ricky Ricardo on the *I Love Lucy* television show, but he was Cuban and I'm not sure he even knew how to ride a horse, let alone make sopaipillas.

We did, however, have the colorful Lee Trevino to look up to and he never denied his heritage. But I wasn't into golf, so I only really saw him on the sports highlights during the 6 o'clock news. Trevino regularly referred to himself as "Super Mex," so there was no way I wasn't going to like this guy. And who couldn't like that other ornery professional golfer named Chi Chi Rodríguez, at least for his first name alone.

Yep, famous Spanish-surnamed celebrity role models were few and far between during my youthful years, so I essentially had to make them up to make myself feel like I was part of mainstream society.

One of my more common inventions was transforming the ever-popular Dean Martin into—you guessed it—Dean Martínez, a common celebrity metamorphosis for many of us around here. Yes, whenever his song "That's Amore" came blasting through on KVSF-AM radio, I would change the opening lyrics to "When the moon hits your eye like a big Frito pie, a la madre. Then they come with the bill and there's no money still, a la madre."

But even old Dean Martínez wasn't the only one of my worldly Hispanic make-believe inventions. The "Say-Hey Kid," also known to many baseball fanatics as the Hall-of-Fame outfielder Willie Mays, was very high on my list of heroes. For a long time, whenever I'd step up to the plate at the Little League fields at what is now known as Salvador Perez Park, it wasn't the home-run-hitting Willie Mays I pretended to be while I swung the bat. Rather, it was Willie Maes, the Chicano slugger from West San Francisco Street. And before Willie Maes there was Yogi Berra, but over here it was Yogi Barela!

Then after baseball practice while I rode my Western Auto stingray bicycle with the banana seat home, I suddenly became "Wheelie Maes," an Evel Knievel wannabe who could sail over winter's leftover potholes with ease.

Of course, a few years later, when quarterback Joe Montana was leading the San Francisco Forty-Niners to multiple Super Bowl titles, he naturally became Joe Montaño in my mind. And the other talented football great, John Elway, was the perfect fit to be renamed John El Buey (pronounced el-WHAY), the Denver Bronco workhorse.

But while the rest of the country was able to enjoy a Super Bowl only one day a year, we locals essentially were able to enjoy a super bowl every week—a super bowl of posole, or a super bowl of beans and chile, or a super bowl of *caldito*.

All the while, however, Hispanics such as Tom Flores and Jim Plunkett needed no identity alterations on my part to make them more like me. But I can blame Flores and Plunkett for making me an Oakland Raiders fan who's gone through decades of misery Super Bowl drought since, the object of taunts like all the others in the Black Hole.

By the time I made it into high school and college, I guess I outgrew the Hispanic makeover of famous celebrities. Otherwise, when the fiery John McEnroe was at the pinnacle of his tennis career, I probably would have called him John Macarena. And NBA great Moses Malone, naturally, would have been Moises Malone in these parts. And the Six Million Dollar Man would forever be the Sixty-Thousand Million Dollars Man, just as the lovable Yoda in *Star Wars* wouldn't miss a beat as Yódale!

We did, however, have plenty of local Hispanic heroes to look up to around here whose names were routinely broadcast across the television and radio airwaves. There was the ever-present Ricky Romero, the hard-busting wrestling champ from Albuquerque, the city that through commercials also made locally famous the musicians "Tiny Morrie, Baby Gaby . . . Al Hurricane," in exactly that order.

And even my own last name made it into the headlines from time to time during those lean times, although for different reasons—"Vigil Held for Peace" or "Vietnam Protesters Hold Vigil." Ironically, there were also other frequent headlines of a Vigil being held, but it had more to do with past extortion shenanigans at the state treasurer's office than with any social movement.

Yes, now we have A-Rod and J-Lo, short for baseball great Alex Rodriguez and actor/singer Jennifer Lopez, whose rear end has been artistically celebrated almost as much as the backside of the historic church in Ranchos de Taos.

Back then Chi Chi and Pancho Rodríguez were famous, but they never called them Chi Chi-Rod or P-Rod. That would have been too nasty! Here in Santa Fe we had basketball legend Bobby Rodríguez, but I don't think anybody would have had the guts to call him B-Rod, at least not to his face.

Times sure have changed, and it seems Hispanic-surnamed people do not feel compelled to change their last names any more to succeed. Still, I wonder if I would have gone any further named Arnold V. Hill.

Try This One Out for Size

I remember the time one of the new exempt bosses at my old state job issued a memorandum to all of us lowly rank-and-files who had been sitting at our editorial desks for well over a decade.

The memo declared that we would all cease and desist using the term "tricultural" in any official capacity when referring to the social makeup of New Mexico, including, of course, Santa Fe.

Most of us scribing cynics, both on professional and personal levels, had already come to the conclusion decades ago that using "tricultural" to describe our city and state was ever so inaccurate. We knew that any time the cliché ever made it into print, dozens of letters followed that were written by conscientious souls who pointed out the radiating rainbow of colors residing throughout our Land of Enchantment.

The term has been the oft-used promotional catch phrase of Santa Fe and New Mexico since way before I could pedal a tricycle. I think the first time I ever registered the phrase being used in a formal way was in the seventh grade during a social studies class with a Mr. Cates at the old Harrington Junior High.

There I sat in Mr. Cates's class on the second floor of the now demolished building one chilly morning in the early 1970s, surrounded by students who were descendants of Native Americans, Chinese, African Americans, Germans, French, English, Lebanese, and who knows what else. And of us local Hispanics, who definitely outnumbered the rest, some like me referred to themselves as Chicano, while others considered themselves Spanish American since the term Hispanic hadn't yet become mainstream.

There we all sat, still sleepy-eyed and waking up, when Mr. Cates proudly declared with his blackboard pointer held high, "Santa Fe is a tricultural city, where Indians, Spanish Americans, and Anglos have lived side by side for centuries!" Boy, were we impressed. Tricultural was catchy and from then on, whenever we could use that phrase to impress someone who wasn't from here, we never hesitated.

Never mind that the phrase wasn't accurate and probably never had been. To our impressionable minds, it was tried and true and besides, everybody else, including our city fathers, passionately used it to impress anybody who would listen. Heck, if other regions could use phrases like "Tri-City" or "Tri-County" to impress someone, why couldn't we use "tricultural?"

A friend of mine, whose parents immigrated to Santa Fe from China in the 1950s, didn't seem to mind when Mr. Cates made his tricultural declaration to all of us wide-eyed impressionables sitting in his classroom. My Asian American friend, who sat right in front of me, surely wasn't Native American or Hispanic, but I honestly never thought of him as an Anglo. Nevertheless, we all considered ourselves quite the unified tricultural group that morning—just because Mr. Cates said so.

It wasn't until my college years that I learned that some Europeans can become mighty upset if you ever refer to them as an Anglo, which technically classifies those who are of English descent. Those of non-English descent, who would otherwise get angry, usually make exceptions when they are called Anglo in New Mexico because over here we're tricultural, even though deep inside we know we're not.

At least in my case, the term "tricultural" went out of style with bell-bottom pants, platform shoes, double-knit shirts, and the affordable Santa Fe house of the mid-1970s. But there it was again, right on a new memorandum in the twenty-first century, reminding me that not all is what it appears to be in the City Different and the Land of Enchantment. The prefix "tri" shall be considered a four-letter word in New Mexico promotion and anyone caught paying tribute to it in any trifling fashion will face the trimember tribunal for trial and tribulation to face a trifecta of punishment.

Instead of letting tri-gones be tri-gones, we were instructed to now use "multi" in place of "tri" in all of our correspondence. I trained myself to refer thereafter to triplex apartments as multiplex dwellings; my kid's tricycle became his multicycle; my trifocal eyeglasses became my multifocal glasses.

Naturally, when I watch old *Star Trek* episodes and Spock refers to his tricorder calculations, I always yell at the TV, "That's multicorder, you Vulcan fool! You may look it, but you all are no longer the tricultural crew of the Enterprise!" Besides, how could the Enterprise have a tricultural crew without any Hispanics? The starship was always a Hispanic short of a tricultural deck.

In reality, though, one day when that trying memorandum was still freshly stuck in my craw, I walked into a Subway sandwich shop on Cordova Road and began looking at the bright overhead menu and BAM!!! There it was again. They were offering the "tri-cold-cut" sandwich. When I thoughtfully pointed out to the teenaged employee that she should talk to her district manager and have the menu changed to read "multi-cold-cut" sandwich, she responded with the cold, blank stare that I deserved. It was only later that I realized that she most likely didn't have time for my tomfoolery because she was multitasking (or doing exactly three things at once) and didn't have time for any more trite customers like me who think they're funny. I can guarantee you the tricultural—I mean multicultural— group behind me in line was not impressed. They just wanted their own tri-cold-cut sandwich so that they could promptly get back to work before three.

Today I'm still grateful for that tricultural memorandum, not only because it gave me fodder for this malarkey, but also because it reminded me of all the other varieties of people in Santa Fe who at face value don't quite fit that tricultural label but somehow don't mind being part of the tricultural mix. They've been triculturized.

I looked forward to another deeply insightful memo from that same boss. But he never did issue us another holier-than-thou memo ordering us to cease and desist referring to New Mexico as a "territory."

Chicanitos vs. Gringitos

When my children were young, I took a moment to go watch them play during their morning recess from elementary school classes. Their teachers and principal had encouraged us parents to observe our kids during such breaks or even to go into their classrooms to watch their teachers in action (something I'm sure the teachers just loved—not!).

To my adult eye, I mostly saw several different packs of kids (the boys) running from one end of the playground to the other in no discernible pattern, while many smaller groups (the girls) gathered near the playground equipment or the fences seemingly in conversation with each other. Every once in a while a ball would fly into the middle of one of these smaller groups and a boy would dart into the gathering to get it, then quickly disappear. All the while, neither group, or so it seemed, acknowledged the other even during the infrequent encounters.

For some reason, what seemed to be chaos to my eye out there on the playground took me back to my own playground days at E. J. Martínez Elementary, the 1969–70 school year to be exact. The school had just undergone its first major expansion, from one rectangular block building with about a dozen or so classrooms to one with a tile-floored gym and a whole wing of fancy new classrooms, which were to be the new digs of grades 1–3.

In addition to the new facility, which also included a library and music room, a whole new gamut of students came along with the expansion. They arrived in a fleet of long, yellow school buses that jammed the front of the school every morning and afternoon, something we existing students had never seen before. I can't really say, in all honesty, if this was the first incident of major redistricting and busing in Santa Fe history, but it was the first I remember.

Before this expansion, I was among just a handful of what were then called "Spanish American" students at the school, which served a mostly Anglo Eastside. But arriving in the buses that first school day in 1969 were mostly other Spanish American children from Galisteo, Cerrillos, Lamy, La Cienega, Cañada de los Alamos, Glorieta, and Pecos. Never before in my short nine-year-old life had I seen so many other children of my same ethnicity in the same place at one time.

But there was also something else I noticed about these new kids: most of them were tough, and they spoke Spanish. They came from what were then some of the most rural communities in Santa Fe County and many of them had to complete their chores, mostly taking care of farm animals or hauling wood and water, both before and after school.

Not all of the new children were Spanish American, however. Some were Texans and some were cowboys, and I learned that year that the two were not automatically synonymous. The bus that came from the direction of Pecos also included a group of large-bodied boys with Texas accents, at least at first, who came from Glorieta. Their folks had recently moved to New Mexico and were employed and living at what was then called the Glorieta Baptist Assembly.

A bus that came from the direction of Lamy also had children whose parents managed or worked on large ranches in that area. Of course, these kids were also tough and a little rough at the edges, if you will. I befriended one of these cowboy kids and I always was fascinated with his nonchalant stories about his teenage brothers getting in fistfights in the bedroom, or getting thrown off a horse into a fence, or how their dad placed a well-targeted boot to one of their behinds for coming in late or not watering the animals. No doubt, I wasn't the only city-slickin' E. J. Martínez veteran at the time who was amazed that there were children being raised in environments so different from our own.

And before you knew it, out on the playground, the commingling of all these cultures began in earnest, but it wasn't as tumultuous as it might seem. First of all, we were all still in grade school, so our first priority was to play. There were only so many minutes in each recess and we didn't have time to dwell on our differences.

After a few weeks of such commingling, however, I remember most of us boys invented a game of tag called "the Chicanos vs. the Gringos." That's right, most of us Spanish Americans who were at E. J. before the buses arrived now started calling ourselves Chicanos and the Anglo boys started calling themselves the Gringos, both monikers I had never really heard on the playground before.

The whole idea of the game was to run around the playground and capture your opponent and take him to a prison area, which was guarded by other members of your group. Meanwhile, the other group did the same. If anyone escaped, then details were sent out to capture the escapee and take him back to the "Chicano" or "Gringo" prison. If the bell rang and you were in prison, you had to report back to captivity at the next recess or a search detail would hunt you down and then tie your shoelaces in knots and bury your sneakers in pea gravel, just in time for the bell.

Now before some of you peace lovers out there start getting yourselves up in arms, remember, this was basically just a game of tag among fourth-, fifth-, and sixth-graders. The amazing thing about this game is that it never followed us into the classroom and it only lasted for a handful of weeks that fall semester in 1969. No lingering hard feelings followed us into the next school year or into junior high.

In fact, some of the Texan boys from Glorieta defected just before Christmas break and they started calling themselves Chicanos, and before you know it, they were running around yelling, "Get the Gringos!" I'm sure the teachers, or any other adult for that matter, who watched us boys play that game in those days saw pretty much the same thing I saw when I watched my own kids on their playground romps. Our adult eyes can see no order in their chaos.

It seems now that the figurative game of tag that occupied so many of our mornings in 1969 actually was an attempt by us grade-school children to make our own social statement. There were plenty of them going around the adult world at the time.

But it quickly just evolved into a regular game of tag that we all soon lost interest in. And the main reason this game lost its luster: We all got to know each other!

Downtown Really Was a Community

It's always a treat for me to listen to the older folks' stories about their own youth in Santa Fe and northern New Mexico.

Most of the time their stories center around the downtown area, which was actually once an honest-to-goodness community with schools, grocery stores, pharmacies, a smattering of dirt roads, and all that other corny, wholesome stuff you see on reruns of *The Andy Griffith Show*.

Even the county jail and city police station were downtown, where the city library is now, right next door to the fire station, where it wasn't uncommon to see the firemen sitting outside watching the slow-moving traffic flow while they waited for their next call.

Sometimes it's hard for me to accept that we've entered into a new era of local Santa Fe, where the long-standing pillars of our onetime village have slowly rearranged themselves adobe by adobe from the Eastside to the frame-and-stucco Southside in only a matter of decades.

The latest example of this is happening right before our eyes with the controversial decision currently on the school board's plate about whether to close a handful of small downtown elementary schools. This move is intended to free up badly needed resources for the "new" local Santa Fe on the south side of town, the only place where young families starting out in the world can afford to live.

I was a grade-schooler when they decided to move both Santa Fe High and St. Michael's High from the downtown area in the mid-1960s, but I was more concerned with catching the next episodes of *Batman* and *Gilligan's Island* than I was with the mass exodus of Santa Fe youth coming of age to the other side of town. If I remember correctly, both Demons and Horsemen were quite excited to be moving into their new digs, as was the community as a whole. Perhaps no one was happier than the downtown merchants, who no longer had to put up with rowdy teenagers en masse on a daily basis.

Luckily, I was part of the second-to-last class of ninth-graders in the mid-1970s who were able to attend solely the old Mid-High School, which occupied the vacated Santa Fe High building—now the home of City Hall. Those were school memories that will last a lifetime, in which they rounded up the young lions from the four public junior-high dens—Harvey, Harrington, Young, and De Vargas—then penned them up together at Mid-High to start them on their way to becoming the Demons of the world. It's no wonder the downtown merchants were always nervous.

It seems that when they closed down Mid-High, most of the other local joints had already closed or soon followed suit: the bakery, Sears, Raul's Restaurant, the Canton Café, Zook's Pharmacy, Moore's clothing store, J. C. Penney's, Payless, Kahn's shoe store, the Plaza Liquors, and surely a lot of others that have slipped my mind. And, of course, the four junior highs themselves are now but smithereens, except perhaps for the shell of Young!

There's no doubt that these local-oriented businesses and schools were the real underlying reason you used to see more locals downtown on a daily basis than you do today. As each one of these longtime stores closed and was either demolished or converted into a gallery or some other tourist-related business, a little chunk of the old Santa Fe died in the process. Most of us were quite unaware of the consequences until way after it happened, our eyes blinded by progress and rising property values.

It's interesting that one of the possibilities school officials are now entertaining is to utilize some of the targeted elementary schools as revenue-generating operations once they've been closed because of their location on prime downtown real estate. So once again, as in our past, truly local places where bona fide residents congregate, most importantly our youth who are in the early stages of developing their own lifelong memories, will be trumped by revenue.

These are hard decisions, especially because so many of the children on the Southside are attending schools with classrooms that are currently bursting at the seams, creating unnecessary burdens on students, teachers, and administrators alike. Who can really blame the parents of Southside students who point their finger in the direction of the mountains and accuse the Eastsiders of "being in their own happy world?"

On the other hand, once we close some of these last public bastions of old-time Santa Fe, are we really telling the future generations of our youth that fond personal childhood memories of the downtown area were just not in the cards for them, even if some of these recollections were as simple and real as visiting a school for a basketball game or a band recital?

Those are exactly my memories of Harvey Junior High, which is now the demolished Herrera First Judicial District Court Building turned brand spanking new county administrative office building. Although I never attended school there, memories of playing basketball games in the cramped gym and fearing some of the kids I thought were roughnecks who did go to school there will be cemented into my mind as long as my brain remains moist. I later got to know the Harvey kids at Mid-High, as well as the students from the other junior highs, and I think we all discovered that there weren't really many differences between us at all, other than our school-district boundaries.

Call me an unrealistic eternal optimist, if you must, but I think most of the elementary kids in school are the same at heart today, only they're probably more concerned with the latest PlayStation release than they are with the consequences of schools closing down or the issue of Eastside versus Southside.

It really isn't until they get older that they begin seeing the differences between them that are mostly put into their heads by other people. It makes me wish we still had that adolescent holding pen called Mid-High, where all the young lions realized without interference that they were more alike than different.

When I think of all the lives that are going to be affected by whatever the school board decides, I thank the Lord that I don't have to make the decision. It's really something that's not going to go away by itself, especially as the Eastside increases in value, thus ensuring that fewer and fewer young families will be able to live there. Multigenerational local residents aren't the only ones becoming quite rare on that side of town. It's also the numbers of children who are decreasing, and the elementary schools in question are suffering the consequences of Santa Fe's prolonged prosperity.

The ABCs of learning once again are being displaced by the 1-2-3s of economics and it's all falling into the same A-B-C pattern of the downtown area—Another Barrio Cleared.

We're All Honkies on the Road

Some time ago, I took my first trip to New York City. I was a simple-hearted New Mexico native going into the bowels of Gotham City, the heart of the lion's den, or so I thought.

Being the naturally tightfisted person I am, with the low travel pay afforded me by my then state job to attend an Internet conference, I got off the airplane at JFK International Airport with one thing in mind: get the cheapest taxi ride into Manhattan that I could find and try not to get mugged in the process.

As I walked through the airport after waiting for my bags, the closer I got to the entrance to the street, the more I saw drivers eager to take my suitcases and more so, I thought suspiciously, my money. As I looked around wondering which driver to pick, a large man in a dark suit emerged from a side door and said, "Come on, I'll take you wherever you want."

"Are you cheaper than these other guys?" I asked him, referring to the many other soliciting cabbies.

"Oh yeah, sure, a lot cheaper," he replied as he quickly picked up one of my suitcases and started heading to the door. I didn't get a chance to ask how much and whether I could get a second quote because all

I could do at that moment was follow my suitcase, which was quickly heading away from me. Before I knew it, I was getting into the back of this guy's large dark Lincoln with tinted windows, and the only thing I managed to ask him in the meantime was whether he could give me a receipt.

"Yeah, sure, I can give you a receipt." Knowing that I would get a receipt eased my mind a little as we headed into the city. As I sat in the back seat of this smooth-riding Lincoln, admiring the Manhattan skyline and having no idea where I was, I couldn't help but think of the many scenes in mob movies where the guy in the back of such a car was being driven to some remote location under a bridge (like the one we were driving over) to get whacked.

As the car headed into the inner-city blocks where the traffic got a little denser, my driver seemed to relax a little more and he made small talk as we waited for traffic lights to change. During such lulls, any time one of the drivers around honked his horn, all the drivers in the vicinity started honking their horns. One minute my driver would be turned around, talking to me, and once he'd hear a horn, he'd abruptly turn around and start pounding on his.

From my vantage, I could never tell why everyone started honking in the first place, and the second that one horn sounded, there were at least five others echoing off the tall New York City buildings in a free-for-all honkfest. This happened not just once but many times during my ride, and I later noticed it numerous other times while I walked on the street. All those car horns honking at once for no apparent reason made me think of a pack of New Mexico dogs. You know, where one dog starts barking, sometimes even more than a mile away, and then every dog within an earshot starts snouting off, passing along the canine news to the nearest unlucky pooch that just happens to be outside at the time.

I have witnessed frenzied honkfests in Santa Fe somewhat similar to those in New York City, however, and they usually occur at the intersection of Cerrillos Road and St. Francis Drive, a proven favorite among town criers. If you're not honking at any of the many sign-wielding demonstrators standing dangerously close to the curb, urging you to honk for their cause, their candidate, or, perhaps, their lack of funds for the day, you're honking at the people on the Santa Fe Southern train (now defunct) or the Rail Runner waving at the cars while it passes through.

If none of these honking catalysts is standing around the curb at the time, you know someone's honking at somebody's bumper sticker. You've seen them, the ones that say "Honk if you've seen La Llorona" or "I brake for hallucinations." I've seen both of those stickers on separate cars, but I think they should be sold and displayed as a special combo.

Now, with the advent of slick computer printers, anyone can make their own bumper stickers, urging you to honk like a New York pro. No doubt, in Santa Fe we have endless possibilities for opinionated honking bumper stickers. "Honk if you think people should keep their dogma on a leash" or, possibly, "Honk if you'd rather have your children play in an arroyo than Frenchy's Field." Others could read, "Honk if the judge who sentenced you became your cellmate" or "Honk if the politician who pounded his sign into your front yard doesn't remember you." How about "Honk if you got laid off from your job so they could pay that Double Dipper"?

For locals, I can imagine some homemade bumper stickers that say "Honk if your Grandpa sold the land" or "Honk if the person who bought your land is now your worst enemy." On the other hand, we could also print up some that say "Honk if your Grandpa stole the land" or "Honk if the Realtor promised they would never block your view."

Some bumper stickers wouldn't urge us to honk at all, but somehow they might compel us to honk anyway. A friend of mine came up with "Skateboarding is not a crime . . . but with proper legislation it can be." And now that the Green Party is in a predicament because of dismal showings in elections, they could print up peppy recruitment stickers that cheer "Go! Go! Go, Green, go!" (That one could be a lot of fun when you repeat it five times as fast as you can, especially at land-grant barbecues up north.)

In all honesty, though, I stopped putting bumper stickers on my car because I got tired of people pointing and honking at me, especially in the drive-thru at Taco Bell. Now, the only bumper sticker I have is invisible and, amazingly, most people seem to see it anyway. It reads "Honk if you think I'm driving like an idiot!" I think that invisible bumper sticker comes stock on all vehicles from the factory at no extra cost.

And speaking of cost, my New York driver did end up giving me a receipt. He handed me some chicken scratch on the back of his business card that barely read $35. They didn't accept that receipt for reimbursement when I got back to work. And boy was I honking mad.

That's How Rumors Get Started

The times were quite trying for the faithful people of Santa Fe when the popular Pope John Paul II passed away. This spiritual leader was able to transcend the Roman Catholic religion, and his down-to-earth influence affected people of different faiths and beliefs worldwide.

When the Pope died, it took me down memory lane to my college days at New Mexico Highlands University in Las Vegas. While I was at

Highlands in the late 1970s and early 1980s, Pope John Paul II had just taken over the helm of the Church. His humble upbringing in Poland, humanistic values, battles against communism, and genuine concern for the poor endeared him immensely to the Roman Catholics of northern New Mexico, who had their own similar histories of intense faith, economic disadvantage, and bouts with discrimination.

At that same time, a college buddy of mine introduced me to his elderly grandparents who lived in Las Vegas. The two were hard-working, extremely generous, and faithful people who had grown up in northern New Mexico during the first half of the 1900s and had seen many changes throughout the decades. It went unsaid that their unbending faith in their Roman Catholic beliefs carried them through many tough situations during their lifetimes. They both mainly conversed in Spanish, which they had spoken all their lives. My friend's grandmother spoke in English more than her husband, who—besides being slightly hard of hearing—struggled to speak to us in broken English and always reverted back to his native tongue, finishing his thoughts in Spanish whether we understood them or not.

His tone usually was serious, but his steely blue eyes often were tinged with a hint of mischief. Even if we didn't know what he was saying half the time, we knew when he was pulling our leg just because of that look in his eyes. Often, it wasn't his words that made us laugh but his furtive glances.

On May 13, 1981, startling news shocked the world. Pope John Paul II, riding in an open vehicle in St. Peter's Square, had been shot in the abdomen by Mehmet Ali Agca. News of the shooting traveled fast throughout the world.

In the small woodstove-heated kitchen of my friend's grandparents, word of the shooting came by telephone. His grandmother answered the ring and the concerned look that overtook her face as the conversation began spoke volumes.

"¿Qué pasa? [What's the matter?]," my friend's grandfather asked her.

She held up her hand to tell him to stop talking so that she could hear. "Uh, uh. Uh, huh," she replied to the caller. "That's just terrible." The woman returned the rotary-dial phone back to its wall mount, and she turned to her husband, who after being waved off by her the first time had turned his undivided attention back to his newspaper.

"Guess what?" she asked him in English. "Judy called, and she said the Pope just got shot."

"Eh?!!" he said, holding his hand up to his ear. "¿Qué dicen? [What did you say?]."

"Judy called to tell us the Pope just got shot," she said in a slightly louder voice.

"Eh?!!" he said again, this time moving his head a little closer to her.

"JUDY CALLED AND SAID, 'THE POPE JUST GOT SHOT,'" she said in an even louder voice.

"Oh, I don't give a good goddamn," he exclaimed back to her in his deep-toned, accented English before going back to his newspaper.

"¡Ave purisima!" she shrieked, tears welling up in her eyes as she made the sign of the cross. "How can you dare say that?" she asked him in Spanish.

"¿Qué?!!! [What?!]," he replied.

"How can you not care that the Pope is dying?" she sternly said to him. "That kind of talk will get you on a hot seat right next to the devil!"

"¿La Papa está enfermo? [The pope is sick?]," he asked her, with a confused look on his face.

"Pues, sí [Well, yes]," she answered. "I just told you Judy called and said, 'The Pope got shot.'"

"Oh, no," he said back to her, this time chuckling. "I thought you said, 'Judy called and said her puppy got a shot!'"

The Pope went on to recover from the shooting, and his close encounter with death made him even more popular around the world. As for my friend's grandparents, well, they recovered from their little misunderstanding. They have since passed away, but they left us with an amusing story about how things sometimes get cloudy in translation.

And that reminds me—I've got to check the calendar and see if it's time for me to take my puppy for a shot.

The City Different Has Many Faces

I couldn't believe my ears when a guy from down south, in Billy the Kid Country, proclaimed he didn't like the adobe/viga look and that he wasn't too enthusiastic about Santa Fe either.

Mike grew up in Capitán and he came to work at *New Mexico Magazine* as a designer and an artist. When he uttered that he felt no affection for the distinctly Southwestern icons that most of us love about Santa Fe and northern New Mexico, I was a little surprised, especially since he was a creative type. And as we all should know by now, numerous talented, creative types have been enamored of Santa Fe and its surroundings for centuries.

Living in Santa Fe and being accustomed to people becoming instantly enchanted with our fair city, I need a wake-up call such as Mike's from time to time. The feeling I picked up from him is that New Mexicans who live outside about a sixty-mile radius of Santa Fe aren't as enthusiastic about the City Different as we'd like to think. Mike, in fact, jumped ship as soon as he could and moved his family to another New Mexico city where he felt more comfortable—Clovis.

In my travels both in New Mexico and out of state, I have found that people elsewhere harbor a big variety of perceptions about what someone from (or who lives in) Santa Fe is all about. I've discovered, for example, that some people in other locales generalize that everyone from Santa Fe is gay or a bohemian artist. Others assume that there aren't any more natives in Santa Fe because of the high cost of living. There was one time I encountered people who thought we Santa Feans were all criminals because the state prison's main facility has been here for decades.

In a KNME-TV *¡Colores!* episode, local writer Carmella Padilla recalled that when she and her husband, *santero* Luís Tapia, told folks in California that they were from Santa Fe, one of them replied, "Oh, so you're rich." The last time I spoke with Carmella, she assured me that she is not rich, but I think I'll ask her for a loan the next time I see her anyway.

Historically, New Mexicans from other parts of the state have had reservations about their capital city, especially when it comes time during legislative sessions to hand out money to communities statewide. There's a perception that Santa Fe gets more than its share of funding for public works projects and especially advertising promotion. I'm sure the New Mexicans who actually travel to Santa Fe for the legislature become even less impressed with our multi-adobe-colored town when they can't find a parking space anywhere near the Capitol and it's just ten minutes until their committee meeting starts. Later, they'll get smacked with their substantial downtown hotel bill after doling out the last of their cash for dinner.

The task of explaining Santa Fe–ness to people didn't get any easier when that book *Santa Fe Originals* came out and a portrait of Ali Mac-Graw graced the cover. As I leafed through that impressive tome, I saw less than a handful of faces that I recognized from my decades of living here. And I saw exactly zero portraits in there of people I might happen to see at Walmart. Incidentally, Carmella is in that book and I'm holding out that I'll see her in Walmart sometime in the future. I'm sure that if she happens to read this, she'll have plenty of original things to say to me while I look for cheese shredders in the household goods section.

I guess I should start hanging out in a better class of joint so that I can get the feeling of what a Santa Fe original is all about. My version of that book would be *Santa Fe Characters*, and we could fill volumes starting with my circle of friends. We may not be too original—we get our jokes from Jay Leno, the Internet, and Tiny's Lounge, just like everybody else—but we all are definitely characters.

Many decades ago *National Geographic* magazine published a feature story about Santa Fe that left many of us locals shaking our heads. Those of us who did not own a hot tub overlooking the Sangre de Cristos or drive a Porsche or eat at the Compound restaurant twice a week felt a little left out. Santa Fe leaves an impression for a variety of reasons and it all stems from *who* you hang out with and *where* you hang out. The writer of that *National Geographic* article obviously never left the downtown area or the swanky Eastside, just like many writers. The writer did, however, go to Chimayó to get a picture of a lowrider—I guess to offer balanced coverage. The *National Geographic* crew had to go there because there was no Walmart in Santa Fe at the time.

Today, it's tough for people to get an accurate picture of what an original Santa Fean is all about. Some of our older neighborhoods no longer have the sense of community they once did, no doubt because of the absence of families with children, families that now can't afford to live in those old neighborhoods. It's tough to get to know your neighbors when they move into the house across the street, make a few cosmetic changes, and then turn around and put the house on the market to make a healthy profit. Now that's not really original, but it doesn't help persuade the skeptics that there's a community of genuine people who still live here and aren't motivated by profit.

Mike, the magazine designer, didn't stick around long enough for me to show him there are aspects of Santa Fe that are still down-to-earth and that adobes and vigas are not just symbols of the affluent but were actually born of real Santa Fe originals way back when.

I wanted to chase him down and tell him before he left, but I didn't want to lose my parking space at the Capitol.

Red and Green, Not Just Stop and Go

There are some things about Santa Fe, and northern New Mexico in general, for that matter, that are quantified in approximations. For instance, nobody really knows for sure the exact year that the Spanish actually founded Santa Fe.

For most of my life, historians told everybody that 1609 was the year Don Pedro de Peralta first established Spanish roots here on official regal orders to replace the previous capital, which was founded at San Gabriel near San Juan Pueblo about ten years before. The year 1609 appeared everywhere—banners, official stationery, history books, tourism brochures, several of my grade school history reports, and so on and so forth. Today, however, the date some people prefer to use for the birth of the City Different is 1607 because of documentation that was discovered years ago. Most people are more than willing to accept the earlier date because 1607 sounds more impressive than 1609—it's older. If we were talking about our own personal age, however, I'm sure most of us would certainly cite the 1609 date because who, besides a nineteen-year-old, wants to be two years older?

Another approximation: nobody really knows where Don Diego de Vargas is buried. Some historians believe he's buried somewhere downtown underneath an old military chapel that was known as La Castrense, which was located "approximately" at the mid-point of the south side of the plaza. If that's the case, then the remains of De Vargas and other unknown historical dignitaries also buried there are eternally resting right next to the new Santa Fe Arcade, which delves down well beyond typical grave level. Doesn't sound very peaceful, does it? Especially for such a giant of New Mexico history and all the other big shots of their time who were deemed prestigious enough to be buried underneath the church. (I won't get into the karma of that one.)

Once I explained to my then grade-school-aged son that the Santa Fe Arcade wasn't really the type of arcade he knows, replete with video games, bowling machines, soda fountains, and other noisemakers. He insisted on going in there anyway to check for himself and he quickly lost interest once he saw all the tourist shops. I'm going out on a limb here, but I think it's safe to say that it's not children who are disturbing the eternal rest of De Vargas—if he's really there.

On the west side of the plaza sits the famous Plaza Restaurant, where, as at all the other restaurants of Santa Fe serving Mexican food, lies another set of approximations on a grand scale. Like when exactly was "Christmas chile" invented? I never heard the term until way into my adult years because when I was a kid, it truly was red or green. You see, all the little old grandmas out there only made one batch at a time. I'm sure there are many theories of how Christmas chile, mixing red and green, came into existence, but I'm sure they all have no exact dates, only approximations.

Personally, I think the concoction was invented at the old La Tertulia Restaurant, where I worked as a busboy during my late high school days and early college years. Christmas chile came about like that old TV commercial that explained exactly how Reese's Peanut Butter Cups were invented. You know, the one where a lackadaisical hillbilly hauling a load of chocolate in his flatbed truck collided with another country bumpkin hauling a load of peanut butter at the only intersection for miles. The country crash resulted in chocolate and peanut butter mixing together on the faces of each of the drivers, who eagerly licked them up.

Meanwhile, back at La Tertulia, there were two swinging doors that connected the kitchen to the dining rooms and also a bus station, and there really wasn't too much maneuvering room inside that old, sprawling adobe building across the street from Guadalupe Church that used to be occupied by Catholic nuns. Then one night (for logistics, let's say during the holidays) a hurried waiter, balancing a plate of red chile enchiladas on one hand and a plate of green chile enchiladas on the other, was making his way to the dining room through one of those swinging doors.

Then suddenly a busboy (I usually say "me" at this point in the story), eager to please a suffering customer demanding more ice water after downing some carne adovada, rushes through the door from the other side and causes it to crash into the waiter. The startled server, whom we'll call Alan for laughs, then spills both red and green enchiladas all over his shirt. After the crash, there is silence, then laughter from the wide-eyed cooks eagerly looking on, and everybody tells the waiter that he looks like a walking Christmas tree. And, voilà, the legend of Christmas chile is born.

I once told this story to an old guy up north and he promptly replied with a barrage of Spanish expletives that sounded like a round of rapid fire from a machine gun in an old World War II movie. He told me Christmas chile has been around these parts for centuries, even before Don Diego de Vargas, and there's even an old Spanish *dicho* that cites Native American legend about it. Now being an amateur at research (among other things), I excitedly asked him to recite the dicho while I took notes. He turned to me very seriously and said, "Navidad para entro, cuatro julio para pasen." Man, that sounded impressive and legitimate too when he said it in his thick Spanish accent.

"What does that mean?" I eagerly asked.

"Christmas going in—Fourth of July coming out," he replied with a serious look.

"Thank you, thank you," I excitedly told him, wondering where I could publish such a newfound treasure. Later I thought to myself, "Wait a minute! Native Americans never celebrated Christmas before the Spanish came and there never was a Fourth of July in colonial times because there was no such thing as the United States yet." I'd been had by a sly old dog and I'm sure I wasn't his first patsy. I wonder how long after we parted company it took him to break out in laughter.

Christmas chile is now big business here in Santa Fe. It generates approximately a lot of money for those who offer it. Former president Bill Clinton ordered enchiladas from an Albuquerque restaurant during his visits to New Mexico and I'm sure his staffers could tell right away if

he ate Christmas chile from the reds and greens splashed on his shirt—
among other stains!

And it's quite possible that President Bush scheduled his holidays in
New Mexico so that he'd be sure to get some of that delicious Christmas
chile "while it's in season." And Al Gore visited several times, but I never
got the lowdown on his Mexican food preferences. But is it true that he
told a crowd of Hispanics during a speech in Española that he invented
tacos? I think Christmas chile would have been the perfect match for
presidential hopeful John Kerry, who visited Santa Fe during his campaign. He could have just ordered Christmas and then he wouldn't have
had to flip-flop between red and green.

One thing that isn't an approximation (or exaggeration) is that the
state legislature (about, uh, some years ago) created the official state
question: Red or green? But remember, that's a loaded question in Las
Vegas because red stands for Robertson High School and green rep-
resents West Las Vegas High School, fierce crosstown rivals. If you're
ever at El Rialto restaurant near the Las Vegas Plaza and the waitress
asks, "Red or green?" just say, "¡Sí!" It's better to play it safe.

Who knows? You just might like the Christmas plate that they serve,
even if it is the Fourth of July.

The Ghost of Christmas Chile Passed

Every year when the wheels of the state legislature race to a halt,
most locals know that parking spaces around town will become somewhat easier to find, at least for a few weeks.

But as the red-colored license plates of the lawmakers leave town
en masse, it's only a matter of time before the specialized placards
are replaced by license plates decorated in a wide variety of hues
that represent most of the states of the union and a handful of neighboring countries.

Yes, here in Santa Fe, we can tell the changing of seasons not only by
the color of foliage on the hardy bushes and trees, or lack thereof, but
also by the color of license plates seen throughout town or up at the ski
basin or up at Chimayó or in Madrid.

There's even an old joke that circulates among some of the old-timers
around here: How can you tell it's late fall in Santa Fe? Answer: Because
the license plates turn yellow again.

And speaking of questions and answers, the state legislature once
actually considered adding the official "state answer" to the books, right
there alongside the official state question, "Red or Green?," which, of
course, pertains to one's preference of chile.

The official answer is none other than "Christmas," a popular combination of both red and green chile. But I don't expect that answer to fly because of all the feathers the word "Christmas" now seems to ruffle, especially at, well, Christmas.

No, the next time the waitress at PC's Restaurant asks me, "Red or green?" when I order my very own *chicharrón* burrito, I'm going to buck the legislature and answer, "I'll have holiday." No doubt she'll first utter, "HUH?!" Then she'll take my green margarita away and go ask the head chicharrón if she should throw me out.

But in all honesty, at my age I've gotten to know my local constitution intimately, and I've learned to never mix the colors of chile anyway. I'm not a gambling man and I know that mixing chile colors is always a crapshoot, especially if good ol' trustworthy Grandma isn't the one who prepared it.

That's right, I'm a chile segregationist and proud of it! When it comes to Christmas chile—bah humbug! I don't particularly care for all those late-night visits from Christmas chile past, or those at the movies either!

In case you're wondering, PC's does not stand for "Politically Correct." So go ahead and order Christmas there all you want. They won't be offended. In fact, there are a lot of colorful characters who frequent the eatery and I'm sure there's occasionally some off-color humor, especially about chile.

And every spring it's time to start planting chile, especially up at Chimayó, where once a classic red-versus-green battle took place over the trademark of Chimayó Chile.

There were those who believed that the trademark should be owned by the community, and they fought until they were red, the same deep color of the *sangre* (blood) that runs through the village. Then there were the people who weren't from the community but had been making money (green) off the name Chimayó Chile, even though it might or might not have come from the village.

There's no doubt that public sentiment fell to the side of the reds, who were passionate and proud about their historically famous chile. If they secure the trademark rights to Chimayó Chile, then the long overdue greenbacks hopefully will migrate to their side. Then, indeed, there will be true Christmas chile in Chimayó, with green all the way to the bank for their red. When and if it happens, call it a holiday over there if you must, but do so at your own risk.

I thought we missed a golden symbolic opportunity when the historic railroad tracks were pulled up from the Santa Fe Railyard during its renovation. I had hoped the City of Santa Fe would donate the uprooted tracks to the county government, which around that time allowed the developer of a new upscale subdivision off NM 599 to build the required 30 percent of affordable housing units in an area away from the much more expensive market-value homes.

The tracks would've served as a symbolic boundary between the two sets of homeowners and maybe even resurrected that oldie-but-goodie term "the other side of the tracks." Who knows, maybe even one of the kids from the market-value side might've stolen away to the other side because he was intrigued by the mariachi music. Then, shazam! We could've had the next Herb Alpert on our hands.

The city, on the other hand, requires that new subdivisions mix the affordable and market-value homes, "red and green, if you will," thus ensuring an ideal "Christmas" community. But the Christmas ordinance sure isn't a holiday for the developers and the market-value buyers, who contend it essentially amounts to a forced subsidy with a long-term potential for decreased property values.

Railroad tracks also played a major part in another "red or green?" dilemma on the other side of the Sangre de Cristo Mountains in Las Vegas. After the railroad brought newfound prosperity to that town in the 1880s, it essentially drove a wedge between the newly arrived Anglo citizens on the east side and the long-entrenched local Hispanic population on the west.

Throughout the following decades, two separate political entities evolved, including separate public-school systems, and the vestiges of that rivalry are still apparent in the two existing high schools: Robertson, whose primary color is red, and West Las Vegas, which sports green. And most of the alumni on each side who keep that hot rivalry alive today, well, they'll never admit it, but they're both the same color now—gray!

Anyway, it's always a joy in the spring to ask whatever new neighbor just moved here from out of state whether I should plant red chile or green chile in my garden. Then I inform him later in the summer that I decided to plant Christmas chile because I just couldn't make up my mind.

When he finally realizes what I'm up to—at about the same time his license plate turns yellow—I ask him if I can borrow a left-handed screwdriver.

By the time he figures that one out, it's usually time for Christmas.

Part 2
Old Santa Fe Trail

Let's just hope that if and when another substantial affordable-housing sub-division gets approved, they don't let one of the confused ones name the streets. We might end up with neighborhood streets with names like Paseo de los Pobres, Penny Pinching Lane, Walmart Way, Vicious Circle, Don Disenfranchised Avenue, Bankruptcy Court, Callecita Pobrecita, Drug Deal Drive, Camino Sin Dinero, Old Santa Fe Trailer, Repossession Road, Beggars Palace, Nada Encantada, Gutter Gate, and . . .

Tourists Say the Darndest Things

There's no questioning the fact that Santa Fe is a tourist town. Almost every day of the year, we locals are reminded that visitors from all over the country come to our fair city to admire our historical standing as well as our pricey mud huts. Now if they would only realize that our traffic laws are more or less the same as where they came from, I'm sure their stay here would be much more enjoyable.

In fact, I was reminded of this one day when I was driving on East De Vargas Street near the Oldest House behind a truck that all of a sudden slowed to nearly a complete stop. And just after the driver veered sharply to the right, I instantly became aware of what caused the delay. A woman was walking right smack in the middle of the one-way street, and in the opposite direction of the one-way arrow.

As I followed the truck's altered path, the woman clearly seemed annoyed that she had to move to the side, where normally anywhere else in America there would have been a sidewalk. But, hey, this is Santa Fe and anyone who's been here a while knows that there are some places in town where a fancy, store-bought sidewalk just isn't going to work, no matter how hard they try.

Not unless they wanted to remove an ancient chunk of the Oldest Church to make one, but there's always the risk of unearthing an unmarked grave in the process. But that might unleash the unworldly wrath of—no, not the ghosts—the historic preservationists, who any developer in town will tell you are much scarier than any old wandering, haunting spirit from the 1600s.

So this lady, by then obviously perturbed at the driver in front, glared at me and barked out in a Southern accent, "Pedestrians have the right of way, you know!"

Hmmm. She was correct, but somehow I just couldn't help but think of someone walking the wrong way down the middle of the one-way Don Gaspar Avenue or Galisteo Street in broad daylight saying the same thing. Bicyclists, yes, but pedestrians, well. . . . Of course, if I dared gun the engine to, let's say, two mph, I didn't see any option except crashing into the Oldest House on the left or into one of the massive stone buttresses of the Oldest Church on the right.

So all I could do was stop, force a smile, and listen to her pointed rants as she tromped by my vehicle while still clearly in the middle of the street. There was no way this lady was going to bring herself to walk on the side of the street, where she might get a speck of soil on her shoes from one of our Old Santa Fe versions of a sidewalk, which most of us know are, well, older than dirt.

Maybe we two drivers had caught this disgruntled visitor on a bad day. She might have woken up on the wrong side of the road. Either that or she just found out how much lodgers tax she had to pay after getting her hotel bill, or maybe she went to an expensive restaurant where they didn't immediately clean her table after she waited a half-hour to be seated and another fifteen minutes to get waited on and then a gratuity was added onto her ticket for a party of, count 'em, one.

And speaking of restaurants, a couple of months ago I went with an old friend, who now lives out of state, to enjoy some spicy New Mexican food at Tia Sophia's, which he had been craving. My friend also brought along his business partner, a nice enough fellow except for one thing—he ordered an enchilada without the chile. Now talk about spotting an out-of-towner a block away, or in the middle of the road, or whatever.

I could see the look in the waiter's eye that he was somehow being cheated. Now our server couldn't ask my new out-of-state friend the sacred question, "Red or green?" and then explain what it means. Man, I have to admit that I had never heard anyone order an enchilada without the chile. With the chile on the side, many times, but never without the chile! I didn't have the heart to tell him that he basically just ordered an expensive taco.

An enchilada without the chile. I guess that's like going to a hot dog stand and ordering a hot dog without the wienie. I can just hear me now on my next vacation: "Yeah, and give me a hot dog—but hold the wienie." I'm liable to get slapped—or arrested, for that matter.

Yep, if ol' Art Linkletter had been a *santafesino*, he might have called his famous show "Tourists Say the Darndest Things." Just ask anyone downtown who deals with them on a daily basis and I'm sure you'll hear some doozies. Like the time my friend Jim told me a tourist came up to him, pointed at the stucco-and-frame Inn at Loretto, and asked curiously, "Do you know how many centuries old that pueblo is?"

Now you know why we locals sometimes have to bite our tongues when we're trying to be helpful, or when trying to pass on the street. But in fall the number of visitors begins to wane, as usually happens after fiesta, and we notice that the license plates begin to turn mostly yellow again, along with the leaves. And there are fewer people in the middle of the street, except, perhaps, in front of the medical cannabis dispensaries, and each and every enchilada will leave the kitchen smothered with chile.

Oh, yeah, and I can order a chile dog again, and they had better not touch that wienie!

It's Not Polite to Point

It's always fascinating when a newborn baby first becomes aware of his surroundings. Even though he's flat on his back or propped up in a baby seat, you can see his little eyes focusing on specific things in the room, each discovery an exciting event to him.

Then before you know it, there's his little hand and fingers wiggling in front of his face and you can tell he's beginning to realize that, indeed, the hand is his own. Later, as the child grows, the hand eventually ends up in his mouth and when it finally comes out, he realizes that he can point to things in the distance and get others to understand what he sees.

From then on, his fingers become an important directional tool, until, of course, his mother tells him it's not polite to point. But finger-pointing is quite an established practice in the human condition. It's been that way around these parts for centuries. Probably the earliest known example of finger-pointing in New Mexico occurred centuries ago when the first Spanish explorers began venturing north in search of gold and other treasures similar to those they'd already pilfered from the Aztec, Toltec, and Mayan civilizations.

When the Spanish confronted the inhabitants at many of the existing pueblos of the time in the mid-1500s, the Pueblo natives used finger-pointing as an effective defense that proved even mightier than the sword. They always pointed their fingers at other native villages and indicated to the Spanish that there were no riches at their own communities but rather at others that always seemed around the bend, over the hill, or across the river. Of course, we all know that the Spanish never found elaborate riches in New Mexico or points both eastward and westward.

Today, ironically, most of the Pueblo natives are bucking centuries of traditional finger-pointing in the other direction. They're now actively pointing the finger toward their own communities, directing those still searching for easy wealth to come partake in the ever-expanding flavors of Native American casino chance. Whether most of the modern gold-diggers are coming away from pueblo casinos empty-handed, much like the first Spanish explorers, is still a subject creating a bit of finger-pointing in and of itself.

Today, another instance of finger-pointing is unfolding before our very eyes. Southeastside Santa Fe residents and their supporters are pointing their fingers away from their neighborhoods and reasoning that there are much better places for affordable housing over yonder on the southwest side.

You know, over the hill, around the bend, and across the river, or somewhere, anywhere but here. But actually, from their vantage point, they can't point east (high-dollar mountainous area) or north (high-dollar historic district) or even south (high-dollar county area).

Yep, the only direction near these parts the Southeastsiders can point to is right down Rodeo Road to the Southwestside, which might soon be renamed Affordableville, or to all us local folks, Villa de Affordable, the working-class suburb of Santa Fe.

It sort of reminds me of the opening scene of one of my favorite movies, *Animal House*. You know, the part where Pinto and Flounder show up at the fraternity party and no matter how hard they try to mingle, they always seem to be directed back to the corner where all the oddball students are sitting.

The idea of affordable housing seems to be turning into the hot-potato issue of our times, and it gets hotter and hotter the farther north and east it gets. Heck, the issue has become so hot, it's getting to the point where only the technical experts can manage to handle it. It's really quite the challenge to catch the hot potato and point the finger in another direction at the same time. Hopefully, this can all be resolved so that all the finger-pointing doesn't turn into finger-throwing.

It seems the only thing that might be able to cool down all the burned, pointed fingers is the issue of water, and it's well known now that doctors advise never to treat burns with water, especially when it's boiling hot.

But as I point back, when I began house hunting many years ago, homes at the $200,000 price category were out of the question for my young family and flying to the moon would have been easier than realizing the $300,000 range. Later, these price categories became "affordable." Heck, I can remember as a twenty-something-year-old when Eldorado was considered the affordable option at prices well below $100,000 and there also were homes galore in that range throughout the city. Whoever said, "What goes up must come down" never had Santa Fe real estate in mind or the psychology of perceived value.

It's just like when Hurricane Katrina hit and there was a general nationwide panic as gasoline reached $3 a gallon. Now I shake my head when I remember people later saying, "That's pretty good," when they referred to the $3.19 a gallon bargain at Sam's Club. At those prices, there was no panic any more, but there was plenty of finger-pointing, especially when someone tried to cut in front of you at the pump.

I know that at these so-called affordable housing price ranges, it's going to take a pretty decent family income to afford these homes and they shouldn't be confused with low-income housing. But people sometimes get the two confused. Let's just hope that if and when another substantial affordable-housing subdivision gets approved, they don't let one of the confused ones name the streets. We might end up with neighborhood streets with names like Paseo de los Pobres, Penny Pinching Lane, Walmart Way, Vicious Circle, Don Disenfranchised Avenue, Bankruptcy Court, Callecita Pobrecita, Drug Deal Drive, Camino Sin Dinero, Old Santa Fe Trailer, Repossession Road, Beggars Palace, Nada Encantada, Gutter Gate, and . . . well, you get my drift.

With street names like this, you can bet (at the casino) there'd be a whole lot of finger-pointing going on—especially at me.

Meeting Beautiful People

Anybody out there want to meet beautiful and interesting people? Now, whether beautiful and interesting people want to meet you is another story, or as we say in northern New Mexico, an enchilada of a different color.

Just a tad more than a handful of years back, there used to be a funny commercial on TV that started out with some happenin', upbeat bongo drumming followed with images of attractive females being escorted by well-groomed men. Then the announcer sounded in with "Meet interesting people!" before he went into a spiel about the rewards of attending the highly lucrative "International School of Bartending."

Every time I saw that commercial, the only "interesting" people whom I could think of meeting as a bartender were the obnoxious ones who become rowdy at last call when it's time to suddenly turn the lights on and inform everybody it's time to get (the hell) out! Or perhaps the inebriated socialite who's perfected the fine art of relentlessly complaining to the bartender that he keeps mixing her Tom Collins wrong until, in frustration, the bartender lets her have his third version of the drink for free. Then, magically, she suddenly becomes satisfied.

But the commercial may have had a point because there is a very small window of time when people do become interesting after a few drinks. I'm sure most bartenders will tell you the window doesn't stay open very long, especially if they're too busy mixing up libations to listen to drunken chatter.

No, rather than attending a school of bartending, my wife and I stumbled upon another interesting way to meet seemingly beautiful and interesting people without going to the bar. And believe me, they literally came right up to our doorstep, whether we wanted them there or not. That's right, average people like us were actually having to shoo-shoo beautiful and interesting people right out the door because, basically, we just didn't want to hear their babble.

And just how, you might be asking at this point, were we able to lure such fortune to our doorstep? We decided to sell our house on our own. Why give 6 percent to a Realtor when we could save ourselves thousands of dollars in the process? Once the word was out that our house was for sale, droves of beautiful and interesting Realtors made it their business to meet us.

My aunt who lives in Albuquerque once told me a story of one particular Realtor she met who chastised her because she related how she successfully sold her own house. The Realtor told my aunt she was actually taking business away from people who depend on home sales for their living and that she, in so many words, should be ashamed of herself. I'm reminded of that story every time I see a Realtor in my neighborhood get out of a Mercedes-Benz or Lexus SUV, then start frantically whaling away with a hammer at a For Sale sign in the front yard of yet another house that's just been flipped.

First I think to myself, "Man, I better stick around because this lady looks like she's going to hurt herself with all that wild whacking. She just might need some help to stop the bleeding and to find the finger she just whacked off and take it to the hospital in a baggie full of ice."

Then I think of my aunt's story and how, because we sold our own home several years ago, we probably took food out of this poor luxury-SUV-driving woman's mouth. Heaven forbid, because of our little amateur home sale, some poor Santa Fe Realtor probably had to forgo the Compound and eat at Lotaburger like the rest of us.

We knew we had to get the house in presentable form, i.e., pull weeds, touch up paint, fix all the odds and ends that I'd been meaning to do since shortly after we moved in ten years earlier. Then we had to get the word out, to the more people the better.

Someone advised that we also should bake cookies just before we had an open house so that the inside would smell pleasant. One of my coworkers told me that when she and her husband were looking for a house, one home seller burned her batch of cookies and the open house smelled like charred dough. Yummy!

As it turned out, we didn't have time to bake for our open houses, so I just went down to the nearest Allsup's and bought some chocolate chip cookies and thoughtfully placed them on a fancy plate in the kitchen so that at least there was the illusion of freshly baked cookies. The power of suggestion would work wonders, I thought.

But none of these basic home-selling tactics is actually what brought the beautiful and interesting people to our front door. What did it was the "For Sale by Owner" ad we placed in the classified ads. Man, as soon as that ad hit the streets, our telephone was ringing off the hook and our doorbell was ding-donging so much, we could never make it to the next commercial while we watched *The Days of Our Lives*.

Potential buyers, you ask? Not a chance! Most of our new suitors were Realtors who all basically told us that we were undertaking a monumental task that would be better left to professionals. One "neighborhood specialist" called on the telephone and said there was no way I had the expertise to match his ability to sell our home. He likened our task to going into a gunfight unarmed, into a food fight without a recipe, into a parking lot with no car. I thought that his particular approach was different from all the others: insult and demean your potential clients until they have no choice but to sign on with you because "you're so good." My oh my, Santa Fe sure has changed!

I got the feeling after about the, um, first interruption of our favorite television soap that most of these beautiful and interesting people stopped being beautiful and interesting once they realized we weren't going to list our home with them. Nearly every one of them said they had buyers they would show our house to once we signed on the dotted line.

Of course, others worked on the greed factor, reiterating time and time again that they could get us tens of thousands of dollars more for our house than we were asking. Now we just didn't pick a figure out of a bag when we decided on a price. We did our neighborhood-comparable research using the same tools that Realtors use. Besides, we didn't want to purposely contribute to the skyrocketing values of Santa Fe real estate and make it even harder for our own children to live here, even though our paltry little conscientious gesture probably amounted to a little more than moot.

No, after that first day of placing that classified ad, we realized that our home ceased being a home and suddenly became a piece of "property" as the flocks of strangers unemotionally wandered through. It's like the time my farming uncle told me he never names any of his cows because some day he will have to either sell them or eat them. It doesn't do you any good to get emotionally attached.

After we sold our house, we sold our car on our own too. I sure hope we didn't take food out of the mouths of any beautiful and interesting used-car salesmen out there. Hungry Realtors now outnumber them, you know, and there are only so many pieces of the pie left to eat.

No Reason to Fear the "Bouncer"

It's amazing how much Santa Fe has grown and changed during my lifetime. Sometimes things that used to be a given are just not as stable anymore. That proud sense of community, which has always been a stronghold among many locals, seems to dilute every time a longtime family home in one of our older neighborhoods is put on the market.

Now, it appears, the new given is that most of these homes are then bought and sold so many times, or maybe "flipped" is the word, that it's hardly worth the effort to get to know the parade of faces that pass through in the process. As more and more of our younger working-class locals are economically phased out of the historic neighborhoods on the north and east sides because of such profit-taking turnovers, sometimes the only real sense of community—à la the old Santa Fe—we have left is in the people.

That's why it's very sad for me when we lose some of our elderly residents. Not only can many of them share with us some remembrances of our once community-oriented town, but just by being themselves, you know they are the old Santa Fe. We lost one of these people with the passing of John "Bouncer" Sena. Not only was Bouncer an authentic local, he influenced multiple generations of Santa Fe children during his lifetime. His many achievements and influences earned him the designation as a Santa Fe Living Treasure in 1990.

Most of us remember Bouncer as "Mr. Sena" from our days at Santa Fe High School. During my time there, he was an assistant principal. Most of the time, a teacher's mere mention of the words "Mr. Sena" was enough to put an end to the unruly shenanigans of some of the wildest, hell-raising Demons at Santa Fe High. Let's face it—what teenager in his right mind would want to be confronted by a large-bodied, intimidating man named Bouncer, just for the fleeting pleasure of making a few classmates snicker at the expense of a teacher?

Sena always explained to his family and friends that his brother told him when they were young that he looked like a bouncer because of his large stature. The nickname stuck. He used his big frame well, especially in 1943, when he was a tackle on the Santa Fe High football team that won the state championship, a feat that wasn't repeated by the school until 1979.

Even long after I graduated from high school, I would see an aging Bouncer around town and would still feel that I'd better not mess around while he was in the vicinity. He just commanded that kind of respect without even trying. Luckily for me, I married a girl who grew up right across the street from him, and as he became more familiar with me being around, I got to know him more as Bouncer the man rather than as Mr. Sena, the enforcer of ornery Demons.

My wife told me that because of the close proximity of her childhood home to his, some teenagers, obviously still smarting from a dose of Bouncer's discipline, would pull pranks and simple acts of vandalism on her family's humble casita, mistakenly thinking it was the Sena household. Years later, I would see Bouncer checking cash-register receipts at Sam's Club, and it was quite a pleasure talking with him about just about anything, knowing that I wasn't in trouble for hurting a teacher's feelings because of some ill-timed wisecrack. It's still a jolt to me not seeing him there talking with everybody and sharing cooking tips while backing up the line in the process.

As I got to know him better, I realized what a small world it was when I learned that my parents' longtime friend Louie was actually Bouncer's older brother. Louie, like Bouncer, was as tough as nails—he was a Bataan Death March survivor—but at the same time he was one of the nicest, most generous and humble people you could ever meet. One day while talking with Bernadette, Bouncer's wife of forty-seven years and more affectionately known to family and friends as Bernie, I also learned that Bouncer's older sister Maria was the original owner and namesake of Maria's restaurant, a Santa Fe institution on Cordova Road. The eatery has changed owners many times, but never its name, and they celebrated her ninety-fifth birthday there in 2010.

It's not too often that one gets to know such an authority figure up close and personal, realizing that this man whom I used to somewhat fear in high school was actually a warm-hearted family man who took pride in setting up hundreds of farolitos around his Casa Solana home every Christmas. Bouncer gave much of his personal time to help, teach, and coach many generations of Santa Fe children, and he devoted just as much of his life to the general community, including two stints as a Santa Fe County commissioner.

It was obvious that Bouncer influenced many people in Santa Fe. Nowhere was it more obvious than at his funeral mass at Guadalupe Church in 2005. Former teachers, administrators, coaches, and local politicians all paid homage to him, including his longtime friend Bob Sweeney, who delivered the eulogy. Sweeney is another living, breathing, walking Santa Fe institution, who has had a Santa Fe elementary school named after him.

A onetime basketball coach of the former College of Santa Fe Knights, Sweeney related to those in attendance that Bouncer used to be the manager of the team. Sweeney said that one time the team was playing another Catholic school, and the game was so important that the archbishop felt compelled to show up. Soon, the fans began forming a long line to kiss the archbishop's ring. For a while, it seemed that people had forgotten there was a basketball game to be played. Sweeney, who was adamant about starting the game on time, complained to Bouncer about what was happening.

"I'll take care of it," Bouncer confidently told him before disappearing into the crowd. Before you knew it, Sweeney said, the crowd dispersed back into the stands, the archbishop put his ring away, Bouncer was on the sidelines, and the game started on time.

I realized after hearing Sweeney's story that if Bouncer could easily disperse a crowd of intensely faithful Catholics, it's no wonder he never had any problem with any of the many generations of mischievous Demons.

The Way We Whir

Every new year, a working scribe feels obligated to write an end-of-the-year wrap-up story or, perhaps, a laundry list of ideological resolutions for the coming year that usually begin to crumble by Valentine's Day or when the Christmas lights finally come down, whichever comes first.

Those of you ardent readers should know some of these seasonal stories quite well, the ones journalists tend to pull out of a hat (or somewhere else) during the slow-news holidays that are full of those cliché-ridden scraps of prose. You know, like "the onset of autumn, the changing of the seasons, the progression of the year," blah, blah, blah. Or how about "Join us as we advance into the twenty-first century," yadda yadda yadda.

Only in my case, the endless routine babble more likely reads like "Join me, as I regress back to the 1960s when people had no choice but to travel through sign-riddled Cerrillos Road on their way to modern Albuquerque, where predictable square city blocks, air conditioning, paved roads, and modern planes, trains, and automobiles took your mind off of the dirt beneath your feet, the monotonous look of mountains and adobe in your eye, the drone of the constant wind blowing against the quaking aspen leaves, and the deafening silence of a dark starry night."

But heck, there are too many things that happen in our neck of the woods to return to the olden days when botulism, scurvy, and, perhaps, airborne radiation clouds purposely released from the Hill could ruin a nice Italian meal, or a gallery opening, or a rica's rocking New Year's party with her best friends.

The days of the deafening silence of a dark starry night might already be a thing of the past in Santa Fe, with the police sirens, the hospital helicopters, the New Year's revelers' firearms, and the light pollution and all. But back when all of these typical urban noisemakers weren't such a factor in Santa Fe, we did hear a low whirring sound comparable to the Taos Hum we hear so much about but never really can hear, at least here in Santa Fe.

Yes, for the past several decades in Santa Fe there was an active whirring noise heard around most of the town and it was probably more pronounced on the east and north sides, where it was downright deafening to some of the longtime residents.

Many informal studies were conducted and we finally learned the source of that annoying drone. It was being created by the collective noise of all the houses being flipped in our popular little town. Heck, in my neighborhood alone, there was one house that was flipped at least five times in the course of just two years.

Man, with all the racket being made by that house-flipping, it reminded me of the times we grade-schoolers would jam playing cards into the spokes of our bicycle wheels to make them whir like the real motorbikes down at Huck's or Bodie's motorcycle shops.

Of course, the mortgage-lending industry and housing market have slowed down dramatically and that raucous Santa Fe whir is a lot less noticeable today. Just as are the car doors and trunks being opened and slammed shut by the blank-eyed visitors who rent many of these flipped houses for a few days at a time so that the speculative investments can help pay for themselves before they sell at a handsome profit.

The city finally cracked down on the phenomenon of drive-thru neighbors, and the whir is being dubbed over with a barely perceivable city crackling sound. Either that or there are so many new infill homes all around the neighborhoods, that new noise we hear might just be the new neighbors' Rice Krispies gurgling from their new kitchen window that's now just inches away from yours.

Some city blocks had more houses flipped than others, and during the constant whirlwind of homes spinning upside-down, the neighborhoods gradually became less neighborly. Another offshoot of the rampant whirring was that it made the traditional barrios way less affordable to those who wanted to sink roots as deep as the neglected Siberian elms in the cracking driveways.

Don't get me wrong, I've flipped quite a few times myself, but it usually was the result of a ski accident, or a change of heart about the politician I voted for, or, perhaps, a few too many beers on New Year's Eve next to a staircase. Sadly, I never profited from such turnarounds and they usually cost me way more than the next unsuspecting bloke, quite the opposite of the profitable City Different flip, the undeniable source of the Santa Fe Whir.

Oh well, not all of our neighborhoods went to the dogs. One year we saw the preservation of a colony of well-rooted prairie dogs just off I-25 that brought the construction of the Rail Runner to a grinding halt.

These cute little critters have a knack for bringing things to an abrupt halt, like the many Little League baseball games that ceased when a baseball got sucked into one of their many holes at Franklin Miles Park. Or how about the softball player's season coming to an abrupt end when his ankle naturally gravitated into a prairie-dog hole while he was chasing down a fly ball just down the street at Carlos Rey Park?

And our beloved prairie dog once was honored by being named the mascot for the future competitive teams at the old College of Santa Fe. But as the luck of the prairie dog's life would have it, shortly thereafter the college itself went bankrupt and had to abruptly close at the end of the semester.

Contrary to the fact that every other Santa Fe athlete considered the prairie dog an additional opponent on the playing field, I wondered if the college's teams would've instead embraced the critter and all of its holes as the proverbial sixth man? If so, they would've been smart to stock up on ankle braces, ice wraps, and extra balls for the opposing teams, who wouldn't be familiar with the lurking holes.

The obvious sports-writing puns about prairie dogs naturally spewed forth in the newspapers, but there was one glaring hole in all of them. They never mentioned the fact that the former Beaver Toyota dealership sat just across the street from the college.

It could've been the start of our newest rivalry in the city, or maybe its newest alliance—the College of Santa Fe Prairie Dogs sponsored by Beaver Toyota. Maybe the two groups of critters would've shared winter's newly formed potholes on St. Michael's Drive and together as brothers brought the hectic traffic to a holy abrupt halt.

Okay, with all this corny punning repeating itself, it's starting to sound a lot like Groundhog Day, which is always upon us so soon after New Year's. Somehow, if the prairie dog's new, revered standing had lasted at the college, I'm sure those pesky critters wouldn't have been afraid to come out of their campus holes when there were people around.

And if they saw their shadows in February, we would have known it was time to get off the couch and go outside and take down the Christmas lights.

Santa Fe Career Advice

In early summer as I see all of the recently graduated youngsters as happy as can be at finishing high school or college or even grade school, it always amazes me that they all seem to be in a rush to get over with whatever level of school they've just finished.

And if they've already come of age, they're probably in a hurry to "get out of this town" and go somewhere else where it's more exciting because "there's nothing happening here." I can remember feeling those same thoughts myself, and then, just as the sun comes up every morning, some old fogey would always tell me, "Enjoy your school years now, sonny, because you're going to miss them when you get to be my age."

Of course, back when you're in high school or even college, you think you're going to live forever, and any words of good advice usually get tossed aside in favor of things that appear more sexy—and later as you think back, much more trivial. And then, inevitably, just as the sun goes down every evening (and suddenly you find yourself in the dark), the light bills start arriving in the mail—only this time with your name on them.

Yes, this time of year always reminds me of the graduation card my dad proudly handed me shortly after I had finished walking down the aisle among about 849 other Santa Fe High School graduates inside Toby Roybal Memorial Gymnasium to shake the hand of the late "Papa Joe" Casados, the principal who doled out our long-awaited diploma. Little did we know then, but that handshake and little piece of paper was actually a powerful, symbolic steel-toed boot, ever at the ready to kick our little immature behinds out of bed and get out there into the real world and quit treating our parents' house like a Holiday Inn and adjoining greasy spoon.

I thanked my pop, ripped open the card, and immediately pocketed the anticipated folding cash inside, lackadaisically there in spirit with him but more enthusiastically looking ahead to a nightlong jaunt of fun and frolic without a concern in the world. It wasn't until days later when I was making a list of who gave me which or what that I noticed the note my wise ol' man wrote inside the card: "Congratulations Son! Remember, you don't eat as much when you have to buy your own food. —Dad."

Boy, those humbling words have never failed to ring true, time and time again. In fact, I always seem to borrow them every time we have a card for a freshly emboldened graduate who has invited us to celebrate his very own symbolic, steel-toed booting into the real world. Obviously, I alter the words from year to year with phrases like "Remember, you don't have all those TV channels when you have to pay the cable bill," or "Remember, you don't take long hot showers when you have to pay the gas and water bills," or "Remember, you don't shop on the plaza all the time when you have to buy your own clothes."

Usually, the words will ring hollow with the confident graduate at first until, of course, the first light bill arrives in their very own name. I've become that old fogey of my youth, offering unsolicited advice at every opportunity, whether the graduating recipient needs (or wants) it or not.

If my wide-eyed graduate is not interested in going to college, which I usually explain opens up much more high-paying career opportunities, I point out some other choices of careers.

"Do you want to do something really cool and make a lot of money?" I'll ask.

"Yes," he might eagerly reply.

"Then go into the air-conditioning field. I hear there's a lot of hot women."

If my impressionable graduate laughs and is still talking to me after that exchange, I'll get serious and tell him that I know of a career that he can get into and pretty much go right to the top.

"What?" he'll ask.

"If you want to get to the top right away, go apply for a job in the roofing business."

Now if I'm not standing there alone after this point and the graduate is still there waiting to hear my next round of career advice, I know this talented youth is well-suited and on his way to becoming an unemployed comedian (either that or a corny bi-monthly columnist who will write just about anything to earn some extra Lotaburger money).

"Really, though, if you think you're a people person, you should go into auto body work," I'll tell him.

"Yeah, why?" he'll ask, usually rolling his eyes.

"Because you'll always meet people by accident."

The long list of career choices and the pros and cons of each can go on and on and they're usually better without the setups. Like, for instance, it's tough to get into supermodel jobs because I hear they're slim pickin's. Get into archaeology or excavation because you'll really dig it, but if you like being the life of the party, go work at the cemetery. Get a job as a pilot because you get to take off a lot. But don't work at the hospital because they'll expect you to come in when you call in sick.

But seriously, watching kids have to go out into the hard, cold world and make their own way has never been easy and it never will be, especially here in Santa Fe, where the same price of a modest "affordable" house will get you nearly twice the house in any other average American city.

All we can do is encourage our youth to be themselves and get into a career that lets them be exactly that. Hopefully, not too many of them will become unemployed comedians who offer career advice.

Living in Spooky Fe

Every Halloween in Santa Fe adds to my fascination with the unfolding story about archaeologists finding skeletal remains all around City Hall when workers razed the old Sweeney Convention Center. Many generations of local Santa Feans spent most of their teenage years attending middle school and high school in that area. And at least in my case, it never occurred to me until all of the digging that for just short of a century, all we Demons from Santa Fe High and later Mid-High were actually romping around above ancient burial grounds.

What a great Santa Fe Halloween irony—generations upon generations of ornery Demons disturbing the eternal sleep of those laid to rest centuries ago. Now if the prior builders found human remains during the last couple of centuries when they were building the old high school (now City Hall) or even the old elementary school that it replaced, well, those discoveries never stirred up any dust at the time. Those probable discoveries just went to the graves with the workers who unearthed them, wherever they are.

But all of us public school brats weren't the only ones irritating the souls of our Santa Fe forebears. The St. Michael's Horsemen down the road near what is now the PERA Building on Old Santa Fe Trail also had a hand in disturbing the peace, at least before 1966. That was the year that most of what was then known as the old St. Michael's College was sold to the State of New Mexico by the Christian Brothers, who still own the San Miguel Chapel and a line of buildings and land across the way on East De Vargas Street. The prime real estate sold to the state is now part of the Capitol Complex, the grounds on which sit the PERA Building, the Lew Wallace and Lamy buildings, and the surrounding parking lots.

Part of this whole 1960s-era real estate deal included a centuries-old cemetery that was located where the PERA Building now sits. Construction workers armed with shovels and bulldozers dug up gravesites from this historic cemetery and reinterred them somewhere else. Many believe there still are undisturbed (and unmarked) gravesites around the area, under the parking lot or the building or who knows where.

I was in elementary school at the time of that PERA site digging. I remember my mom telling relatives that during the construction phase workers unearthed a coffin that was still in pristine condition.

Inside, they found the remains of an unidentified woman whose well-preserved body was cloaked in an 1800s-period dress. She wore an embroidered shawl that appeared to be brand new.

Later, after the PERA Building was erected, custodians and other state employees working late at night often reported that they would see an apparition of a woman on the fifth floor and that she would disappear, sometimes through walls, when they approached her—sort of like the employees at the old Furrows hardware store. The general consensus at the time was that the ghostly figure was that of the peculiar woman found in the pristine coffin.

You could drive yourself batty thinking about all the creepy stuff in that area, also known as the Barrio de Analco, which today many call the "oldest neighborhood in the United States" even though it's been quite a long time since it's been a neighborhood. It also was the site of many violent deaths of Spanish and mestizo settlers who were killed by Pueblo Indians during the Pueblo Revolt of 1680. No doubt there are plenty of unmarked graves in Barrio de Analco that were placed there long before the first person was ever laid to rest in the nearby cemetery below and around the PERA Building.

Every January when the state legislature is in session, I can envision the wandering souls uprooted from this area cemetery forever roaming the grounds looking for what used to be their final resting place. No, wait . . . I'm sorry, those are the droves of cars cruising the parking lot looking for a place to park.

We've gotten used to our cemeteries in Santa Fe being uprooted, just like the one behind Dunkin' Donuts and the next-door Firestone tire shop. I'm sure a few gravesites were uprooted when they built these businesses, which also utilize holes for their existence. And we can never turn a blind eye to those beloved prairie dogs that were discovered to be uprooting human bones from gravesites at that old Fairview Cemetery on Cerrillos Road next to the deaf school.

Yes, growing up in a historic place like Santa Fe, you kind of get used to bones and burial sites getting uncovered nearly every time someone decides to dig a hole. I guess the trick is not to dig too deep, unless you want trouble, just like journalism.

A few days after I noticed a hardy rainstorm drenching the exposed southern adobe wall of the "Oldest House in the USA" in the Barrio de Analco, I stepped into the business to jokingly ask the former proprietors, Suzanne Alba and her mother, the late Elvie Vigil-Ogard, whether any of the ghosts inside would escape if the rain melted a hole in the wall?

On that crack, Suzanne revealed that she often felt an otherworldly presence in the old structure, even during the day, and sometimes objects she knew were in a certain place when she left at night were mysteriously repositioned when she returned in the morning. In fact, she said that one time a self-proclaimed clairvoyant walked in the shop and told her there were a couple of spirits making the rounds in a triangle between the Oldest House, the San Miguel Chapel (a.k.a. the Oldest Church) and an old building that housed an antique shop across the street on the southwest corner of East De Vargas Street and Old Santa Fe Trail.

The woman told Suzanne one of the spirits was an evil one, probably a woman, and the other was an old Native American man who actually protected them from the other, malcontented spook. "She told me, 'In fact, he's standing behind you right now,'" Suzanne said the clairvoyant pointed out to her in the shop.

I guess if you think about something too much, especially all those skeletons in the closet, it's enough to drive you bonkers. Although both Suzanne and Elvie admitted there could be supernatural forces at work, neither one of them ever felt threatened or scared inside the building, which is owned by the entity that operates St. Michael's High School and other properties in the Barrio de Analco. At that point, I realized I was getting way more information than I really wanted to hear. Sometimes I had to walk those same streets to get to and from work and I didn't want any more scary details to add to my ghostly insecurities, especially with more legislative sessions coming up.

Some years ago, headlines were made when workers unearthed human remains on Kearny Avenue and the whole project was put on hold until first the police, then the archaeologists could determine whether anything suspicious had taken place. Fortunately, if I can recall correctly, they determined a proper burial occurred there more than a century ago right below the old Fort Marcy military complex in a makeshift potter's field, a public burial ground for poor or unidentified people. Either that or someone just buried their grandpa in the front yard, as people routinely did in the old days.

It's been said that even more human remains were found in the summer of 2008 in another previously unknown potter's field on the grounds of the Basilica Cathedral of St. Francis. Tight-lipped archaeologists supposedly analyzed the subsurface near the city-leased parking lot just west of the old St. Francis School, and more than likely on part of the site of an ambitious, proposed development. No wonder I never wanted to park there! (But seriously, it was really that I didn't want to pay to park, more than anything else.) And yet in all my years of growing up here, I never knew that there are also remains all around and even underneath the St. Francis Cathedral. Earlier, as part of an assignment for an issue of *New Mexico Magazine*, I had the privilege of accompanying (Santa Fe–born but now Dallas-resident) documentary filmmaker E. Anthony Martínez into the crawlspace underneath the west-side pews in front of the altar of the 160-plus-year-old church.

The Basilica Cathedral was built around and over older colonial and Mexican period churches on the same site. And as any aficionado of New Mexican churches knows, people were always buried in cemeteries situated around church perimeters, with the bigshots getting the choice digs underneath the church-interior floorboards and the courtyards in front of the church.

That's right, yours truly and Martínez, who filmed the documentary *Corazón de Santa Fé* for the Basilica Cathedral as part of Santa Fe's 400th anniversary celebration, photographed and filmed unidentified human remains that were unearthed during a pillar-renovation project in the 1950s or '60s. Much of this area covers the old cemetery, and scores, if not hundreds, of unidentified and unmarked graves from the 1600s, 1700s, and 1800s remain.

We also documented a metallic urn, which was adorned with dried roses and a memorial pamphlet with the name and photo of Andre V. Johnson (Jan. 29, 1976–May 2004). It reportedly contains the cremains of a man who requested that they be placed next to the permanently sealed, concrete tomb of Archbishop Jean-Baptiste Lamy, who rests underneath the southwest section of the altar along with the remains of two other archbishops. Although unverified, it's also said that right next to them on the south side of the altar are the remains of Gertudis Barcelo, a.k.a Doña Tules, proprietor of a prosperous gambling hall and house of ill repute during the American occupation and conquest of Santa Fe in the 1840s and '50s.

Man, until now, I never realized that throughout my life I have been tromping over human remains throughout Santa Fe on a daily basis. Way back when, I used to take my out-of-state college buddies over to glimpse the old coffin at the Oldest House as well as what I told them was the "oldest" wooden Indian in the country, which used to greet visitors outside. (The old carving mysteriously disappeared years ago, by the way.)

When it comes to spooks, I prefer to stick to good old La Llorona. I've chosen to place her right up there alongside Santa Claus. That's right. They're both characters that our parents used to make us behave when we were kids. You know, if you don't behave, Santa *won't come* see you, or, if you don't behave, La Llorona *will come* see you. But there comes a time in our lives when we get older and begrudgingly realize that these stories just aren't real.

And in La Llorona's case, I'm still waiting for that moment to arrive.

Thanks for the Memories

I guess Memorial Day is as good a day as any to get forgetful, even though it might not be the real Memorial Day but the "observed" one. I still can't get it straight whether the actual Memorial Day falls on May 29, 30, or 31. I know they taught me the real day sometime back in the third grade, or was it the fourth?

This guy I know was squirming on the witness stand once and a defense attorney pointedly asked him where he was on the night of the 28th. He calmly looked back and said, "Sir, I can't even remember the date of my anniversary. How do you expect me to remember the 28th?" Boy, if that guy consistently couldn't remember the exact date of his anniversary, it's no wonder he wasn't overly intimidated by a persistent three-piece-suit-wearing lawyer who undoubtedly enjoyed making people uneasy under pressure. I'm convinced my friend's wife made his life way more uncomfortable once a year around anniversary time or, come to think of it, probably again around her birthday or Mother's Day.

Being forgetful is especially memorable on Memorial Day of all days, even though it doesn't always fall on the day it's supposed to. That old song lyric "Everybody's working for the weekend" applies to holidays too—especially the camping holidays.

Apparently the people who put on Indian Market forgot that the festival usually falls on the third weekend of August, except one year it fell on the fourth weekend, I think. Usually I'm lucky to remember to get out of town on the third weekend to avoid the downtown crowds, but if I forget, then I'll come back home to find even less parking the following weekend.

Yep, on any given Memorial Day weekend we'll see more action than usual at the local and national cemeteries, where people from all over come to Santa Fe to remember their interred loved ones. I've got many aunts and uncles as well as a grandma and grandpa buried at the National Cemetery off North Guadalupe Street, and I never can remember the locations of their final resting places, Memorial Day or not.

You'll usually see me, along with many others in the same predicament I'm sure, traipsing around the rows of white gravestones in search of a familiar name. And more times than not, once I've found the marker, it's nowhere near where I first thought it was. And it's even more confusing with those gravesites that are marked with the flat markers, which were used during a federal cost-saving period when they declared the government couldn't afford the upright white markers anymore, or whatever reason they came up with.

One thing I do remember, however, was the day they held services there for my uncle, a veteran of the Korean Conflict with a tremendous sense of humor, not to mention a huge influence on me. After the cemetery officials shooed us away from the open-walled hillside memorial chapel because there was another veteran funeral right behind us, a few of us cousins hung around to glimpse my uncle's actual gravesite while everybody else hurried to their cars.

Luckily, an observant cousin of mine was watching the cemetery workers because he noticed one of them had inadvertently switched my uncle's gravesite-identification number with the veteran's whose memorial service was held before ours. That meant that their freshly covered graves might have been misidentified for eternity, a final symbolic prank of my uncle's on his wife—and he pulled many on her in his lifetime, much to her chagrin.

You see, a veteran's spouse is laid to rest on top of him or her in the same plot after they both have passed away. I'm sure my uncle would have had his usual boyish grin when people realized that his final act of tomfoolery would have had his widow laid to rest on top of his next-hole neighbor, while a strange woman was eventually placed on top of him. But, to his credit, I think he always remembered their anniversary.

Nevertheless, my cousin prevented such an occurrence because he and the rest of us refused to be hurried away, all of us intent on seeing the exact location of his grave, which we surely would have trouble finding later. But then again I often wonder if the numbers were truly placed on the right spots after all and, really, if this was just an isolated incident. You see, even cemetery workers are forgetful, Memorial Day or not.

I guess it's understandable that we can't remember simple things on Memorial Day, like the mayor not being able to answer his constituents which came first, the city or the acequia madre, because there can't be a birth without a mother. Or how about the distressed single mother with buckets on the floor who couldn't remember if her skylights leaked before or after the roofer came and sold her a brand new roof that still didn't fix the leak?

I heard someone joking in the locker room the other day saying the one good thing about dementia is that "you meet new friends every day." That's pretty good, because maybe a slight bout with dementia could make me forget about all the things I remember that upset me and I wish I couldn't recall.

But, then again, if I couldn't remember all those insignificant details about life in Santa Fe, I'd have zero *chisme* for cheesy columns that don't seem to flow in a linear pattern—sort of like the mysterious path water takes through a leaky skylight down through the ceiling and across the viga to the wall and into the bucket as well as the floor.

Therefore, to all you prospective grooms out there who will sit silent while your fiancée and her mother contemplate an exact date for you to later unwittingly forget on the witness stand, speak up now or forever hold your peace. And whatever you decide, don't let them pick Memorial Day for the happiest day of your life because, as we've already been through, it never falls on the same day the next year. You'll never remember, and you'll never win—regular occurrences you'll soon be getting used to.

On second thought, Memorial Day might be a good anniversary date because then you'll have a valid excuse when you forget. You'll just have to pull out last year's calendar and point to the 27th, or was that the 28th?

Imagine and You Shall See

When I was just a tyke in elementary school, I remember the first time my mom told me about being able to see the horse's head going up the mountain. "Oh yeah," I thought to myself every time the subject came up, either with her or somebody else, "the horse's head going up the mountain."

Of course, she was referring to the rough outline of aspen trees and mountain contours that formed the general figure of a rounded horse's head below the Santa Fe ski basin pointing up toward the open-faced Big Tesuque. But, honestly, at the time, I never really could see the horse when I was younger, at least not until somebody pointed it out to me in a photograph later on in life and I was able to let go and imagine.

One time a coworker of mine asked me to point out the horse's head from a clear vantage point of the mountains from our office. After about five painstaking minutes of my trying to point, draw on the ground, and explain, she still couldn't see it.

Then it dawned on me: the surrounding evergreens have grown so much around the aspen-head outline that it really doesn't look much like a head anymore, or anything else for that matter. We had to go inside and find a vintage photograph of Big Tesuque so that I could point it out to her—and she still couldn't see it, even with my short, scarred finger outlining and pointing right at it!

But there was one peculiar thing that struck me about that incident, and that was, I could still clearly see the head, even today, despite all the new growth. It took my having to look at the mountain with a clear mind and some fresh eyes to realize the horse's image is slowly but surely disappearing and it's not as obvious as it used to be. It was sort of a "The emperor has no clothes" sort of thing.

I hate to admit it, but maybe that's the plight of Old Santa Fe. There is still a whole bunch of us locals out there who can still see it, but to some fresh eyes, it's just not there, or at least not as prominent. Of course, it all depends on your definition of "Old Santa Fe." For many of our kids, unfortunately, their definition of Old Santa Fe is Villa Linda Mall (no longer), the Sweeney Convention Center (no longer), Toys 'R' Us (no longer), and . . . well, you get my drift.

Another friend of mine, who grew up in the Nambé Valley, told me that from that northern vantage of the Sangre de Cristos, an outline of an eagle in the aspen trees just below the south side of Santa Fe Baldy was clearly visible during his youth. In fact, he said, the now closed elementary school in Nambé took on the mountainside eagle as its mascot.

He tried to point it out to me during one of our past northern excursions, but just as my coworker was blind to the horse's head, I couldn't see the bird, no matter how hard I tried. The surrounding evergreen growth has also closed in on the image.

Obviously, to my friend, the eagle is still there clear as day. Despite the new growth, beak and outstretched wing point north toward the majestic Pecos Baldy and Truchas Peaks, inspiring all the little eagles of Nambé Valley past to try their hardest. In old photographs of El Rancho and the Pojoaque Valley looking east toward the mountains, the eagle is hard to miss, with a little imagination, that is, and some say it still reminds them more of a thunderbird.

And just farther north on the same Sangre de Cristo chain, in an outline within the evergreens below Trampas Peak, there's an *S* on the mountainside that looks uncannily similar to the *S* on the chest of the comic-book hero Superman. I've heard some people call it Superman Mountain, but I prefer to say that Superman is really from Trampas Peak and he gets his power from the Sangre de Cristo Mountains, just as many of us do. It's only a matter of time before this image is also overtaken by growth.

Historians will tell you that all of these figures of local lore were made possible by an unattended campfire that originated in Hyde Park in the early 1900s, and it burned through the western Sangre de Cristo Mountains from there all the way north through the mountains to Peñasco. Back then, they didn't rush out the door to put out the fires, because of limited resources and technology. It was treated just as a usual occurrence in the forest.

The open space created by the burn made it an ideal environment for aspen trees, which do best on steep, well-drained slopes with lots of sun. But now that the slower-growing evergreens are starting to come of age and encroach on the quaking, sun-loving trees whose natural growth cycle is coming to an end, the face of our treasured mountains is slowly reconfiguring itself right before our eyes.

Back in the day, people had more time (or at least they made time) to look up to the mountains and imagine. Maybe as our mountains change before our eyes, there will be new figures to inspire us and our children, who probably think we're nuts when we point out things they just can't see.

Now in my later years, I've learned of at least one new mountain apparition born of smoke, or mist, or even swirling snow up at the Santa Fe ski area right near the horse's head. I met a snow maker/snow groomer up there who told me of a new legend on the slopes, the Chainman. This is an apparition of what appears to be a skeleton head that only harrowingly reveals itself to someone who talks smack about it and doesn't believe. A new friend, Dennis García, who has worked up there seasonally for many years, said other snow groomers told him about Chainman when he first started working there.

Dennis said he scoffed at the idea of a smoky skeleton, although he admitted that working up there at night does leave plenty of room for the imagination to run wild. At night on the mountaintop, there are awesome views of the city lights of Santa Fe, as well as Los Alamos, Española, Pojoaque, and even Moriarty, Estancia, Bernalillo, and Rio Rancho, among all the other little communities.

So later on that first year he worked, Dennis brought his camera up to get an inspired picture of the darkened view. When he got the pictures back later, there, clear as day, was an orb on one of the pictures. It was the Chainman and he looked like the skull of Darth Vader, helmet and all. Dennis says he never said anything bad about the Chainman from then on and neither did any of the other snow groomers who also worked at night.

After learning of Dennis's experience, I made sure I told my kids that if they talked trash about the horse's head, the eagle, or, later on, Superman's S even when it's no longer visible, they're going to get a visit from the Chainman because they don't believe. It'll be the northern New Mexico version of that other famous horse's head—you know, that one that showed up in the Hollywood producer's bed in *The Godfather*.

Except our fabled Sangre de Cristo horse's head is real and it predates the make-believe Hollywood one.

Alfalfa Fields and Affordable Casas

I often wonder what Santa Fe will be like when (and if) I make it into my later walker-assisted years. I wonder not so much to satisfy my own nervous curiosity, but I'm more anxious about what it will be like for my own children.

When I was growing up, it seemed like a given that I would get a job, buy a house, and be able to settle in my hometown without any real obstacles other than showing up to work every day to earn money to pay the bills. Of course, I really didn't get serious about settling down until I was well into my late twenties, and after I finally got into the property game, I quickly realized that I should have gotten into it much earlier than I did because I would have saved thousands of dollars in the process and maybe made some money in the long run.

That familiar scenario of the American dream of home ownership was well within reach for many of my New Mexican ancestors, albeit a New Mexican variation of that theme. In the past, most newlyweds were bequeathed a small parcel of land, usually from the family acreage, and then shortly after the priest gave them their nuptial blessings, they started making their own adobes—even the bride! And before you knew it, voilà, a casita sprouted up on what used to be a perennial alfalfa field. As the family started to grow, each year friends and family would pitch in and add another room for a new little one and, as they say, the sky was the limit. It wasn't unusual for some grandmas and grandpas to produce fifteen, maybe twenty children and still have plenty of alfalfa fields for each one of them, and perhaps for a favorite grandchild or two.

Undoubtedly, it's been a long, long time since any of these types of family transfers occurred in Santa Fe, especially one without a Realtor, a mortgage company, a neighborhood association, and an arm and leg involved. Living in Santa Fe today, I'm afraid that I'm fresh out of family alfalfa fields to give my children, but I can offer them a Tuff Shed, a small plot where some lilac bushes now sit, and our mortgage balance. Some will argue for me to quit whining and go out and grab the opportunities that are still out there waiting to be grabbed. They're right. That's why I write. But, unfortunately, the pay to write this poppycock barely covers the family's biweekly Lotaburger tab and is nowhere near the ballpark to get a family alfalfa field of our own.

Come to think of it, I've never actually seen an alfalfa field in Santa Fe during my whole life here, although I have seen an outhouse or two—but not since high school. Back then, it was a rite of passage for the SFHS Demon underclassmen to steal an outhouse for the homecoming bonfire. I think the last one I actually remember seeing was at a home in the area where the state treasurer's office now sits, right off of south Galisteo Street.

I'd like to go back in time and see if that long-gone but not forgotten outhouse was actually located on the grounds of the treasurer's building. Talk about a poltergeist moment. Now that's a lucrative opportunity out there ready to be seized. I could run for the high-paying state-treasurer post next time around. On second thought, maybe not. With my last name and all, I doubt I'd have much of a chance. And for those of you out there who are wondering—no, we're not related, me and the former state treasurer Robert Vigil who served time in the pokey for malfeasance in office. Otherwise, I'd probably be working there making good bucks, enough to afford an alfalfa field, and I wouldn't have to be writing for *Journal North* readers every two weeks.

Yes, for all of us Santa Fe locals living paycheck to paycheck, there might be some light at the end of the cul-de-sac. The city council's approval of the 30 percent affordable-housing ratio for all new developments seemed like a well-intentioned gesture toward our common lack of alfalfa fields.

Too bad so many of the developers, contractors, and people who otherwise profit from such new developments are so opposed to the affordable housing provision. Now we just can't go out there and let people start making their own adobes again, can we? Three modest, affordable homes out of ten doesn't seem like much to gripe about, but hey, someone should tell these guys that the maid, the butler, and the gardener need to live somewhere.

It's kind of fun to dream about having a whole line of alfalfa fields to leave to each one of my children so that they can start their own slew of little sprouts. About the closest thing to an alfalfa field in Santa Fe nowadays is the Santa Fe Farmers Market at the Railyard and the rodeo grounds, and most of that homegrown alfalfa comes from outside the city limits. Even if I could afford an alfalfa field in Santa Fe, there wouldn't be any water to irrigate it. Today, it appears that the only locals assured of (ball) fields to pass onto their children are the prairie dogs, and they don't even have to make their own adobes. They just have to burrow another tunnel in a grassy field and the sky's the limit.

Oh well, I guess my children are going to have to be resourceful if they want to live in Santa Fe when they get older. The way things are going, to borrow from Frank Sinatra, if they can make it here, they'll be able to make it anywhere.

Tuning in to Spanish

Back in my pre-elementary-school days, my good ol' ma sent me to live with my aunt and uncle in the remote Taos County village of Vadito in the Sangre de Cristo Mountains of northern New Mexico. She shipped me off because everyone else in my immediate family was either working or going to school, and there was no one at home during the day in Santa Fe to take care of me. You know, make sure I didn't get myself into any trouble with stick matches, the telephone, the stove, my sister's cat, or down at the Boys Club, perhaps.

It had been quite a few years since my aunt and uncle had had little ones around in their pitched-tin-roof adobe house, let alone a little nose-pickin' brat who was hungry all the time. All their daughters were already married and had moved away, were in college, or were just finishing up high school.

One of the first things my new immediate family learned by having me around full-time was that five-year-olds tend to repeat things they hear, even the delicate things they don't quite understand yet. Yes, a five-year-old repeating things he shouldn't makes for quite a few awkward moments for the adults, especially after the company arrives.

But my mom's sister and her husband were quite resourceful people and they came up with the perfect solution to dealing with a living, breathing tape recorder that spouted off at the wrong times. Whenever a sensitive subject came up, they started talking to each other in Spanish, so that first, I wouldn't understand, and second, I wouldn't be able to repeat anything to the guests.

The couple often talked Spanish with each other and their friends, but they spoke mainly English with me because that was the only language I knew at the time. I was one of those second- or third-generation Hispanics who was raised speaking English only because our parents didn't want us to go through the same language barriers they went through as Spanish-speaking children adjusting to English-only schools.

But my aunt and uncle's daughters also knew Spanish. They learned it before this little English-only speaker from the big city of Santa Fe arrived on the dirt road in a green four-door '57 Chevy. The little village of Vadito along the High Road to Taos was still isolated enough that you didn't need to speak English everywhere you went, unlike in Santa Fe.

The girls, when they were home, were also careful to talk only Spanish in front of me because they knew I was already especially adept at bringing up sensitive subjects around their boyfriends, who, of course, egged me on to blab even more. That's likely the first time in my life when I found out—the hard way—that girls could pinch pretty hard when they're angry. Yep, those painted-fingernail pinches on the arm probably would have hurt a lot more if the pain wasn't somewhat dulled by their boyfriends' laughter, which seemed to re-energize me.

Of course, the visiting beaus also felt the wrath of the *primas* if they had too good a good time at the girls' expense. I think for a while there the girls wouldn't let me into the same room when the boyfriends came to visit for fear that this happy-go-lucky *chamaco* (ornery boy) would once again get all the guys in the room in trouble. In fact, back at home, I had my own oldest sister's boyfriend trained to bring me candy bars so that I would go away and leave them to their shenanigans. "No candy, no peace" was my pre-school mantra.

I guess not much has changed with me some fifty-plus years later. It seems that a lot of places I go, people clam up in front of me out of fear that I will repeat what they say in this column. "Hey, don't say anything in front of Arnold or he'll put it in the paper" is what I used to hear. (Of course, when I do repeat something overheard, I'm sure to do it out of pinching range.) If only they knew that just a few years ago all they had to do was talk in Spanish and they could rest assured that anything confidential discussed in my presence would never make it into print, at least in English.

But I have to say that my Spanish is getting better and better in my older years. In fact, it's getting so good that now they're not messing up my orders as much down at the Lotaburger. Yes, by the time I get home, I can rest assured that them papas fritas are in the bag and there's no need to go all the way back to get them, or that second meat patty either.

In fact, I can now say that I speak Spanish "effluently." That is, I've learned most of the cuss words and, of course, the words Spanish speakers use when I suspect they're talking about me. I'm still working on dropping the "ef" and just speaking fluently so that I can communicate beyond my food order. Now that I mention it, I think I talk a little effluently in German, French, and even the Keres language, thanks to some of my San Felipe Pueblo friends in college who were no doubt talking about me every time they started pointing at me and suddenly broke out laughing in their native tongue in the middle of a beer bust.

Let's see, I think I just heard some people talking about me in Spanish on my way to write this column, so I better go look up the words I'm sure I heard them use: *bonito, listo, fuerte, muy macho, okeydokey,* etc. All right, I know all you real Spanish speakers out there know I left out all the words that they more than likely used when they talked about me, like *mentiroso, tonto, loco, pinche, borracho,* or *baboso.* That's right, even in different languages we tend to see ourselves in a different light than others see us.

Oh yeah, and if any of you have a rapid-repeating five-year-old that you just sat down in the corner to take a time-out moments ago for blabbing out the wrong thing at the wrong time, you just might have a budding cheesy-writing journalist on your hands.

Perry Como Said Llama

I received an interesting email from a fairly new reader who told me that he's been living in Santa Fe for less than a year and these columns have been catching his eye of late. Although he did write that he enjoys reading them, there was one catch: he didn't always understand them.

"This is true, even though I don't understand it sometimes," my new friend Frank writes. "In your August 4 column, for example, you mention 'when the Kiwanis guys are taking their sweet time about torching Zozobra.' Is this a secret initiation rite within Kiwanis, or is it something peculiarly New Mexican?"

Hmmm, I guess from the timing of Frank's move and September's La Fiesta de Santa Fe, he must have arrived after last year's burning of Zozobra. That decades-old torching ritual is kind of hard for anyone to miss around here, even if you don't go anywhere near Fort Marcy Ballpark. And many locals do, indeed, avoid going there, mostly because of the crowds (and probably now the initiations).

I really don't know if there are any secret initiation rites within the local Kiwanis Club around the burning of Zozobra, but in the seemingly long time it takes to wait in line, get searched, then find a place on the field to perch, etc., there just might be enough time for the Kiwanis dudes to get in some behind-the-scenes initiations before the show starts and possibly some after the lights go off.

I've heard a thing or two about such secret initiations, and about the only one I can think of is that one at the beginning of the movie *Animal House*, where the cloaked, smirking Omegas are having some masochistic fun at the expense of their new fraternity recruits. Yep, that's where I picked up that classic line that I used to repeat often before our full staff meetings during the day: WHACK! "Thank you, sir, may I have another?" WHACK! "Thank you, sir, may I have another?" WHACK! . . .

I don't know about you, but now because of Frank's curiosity I'll never be able to hear Zozobra's groans in the same light again—WHACK!

But my new friend had some more questions for me to answer, and I'm sure these aren't the typical exchanges you hear down at the local visitor center or on the tour-guide trolley or at an eager Realtor's open house.

"And '*pinche como se llama*' . . . it's 'What's your name?' with a twist, but what twist?" Frank wonders. "Maybe I'll understand these things after I've been living here for a while."

Well, to Frank and all my other newly arrived friends, over in these parts (and once upon a time a long, long while ago on the Eastside), *Como se llama* not only means "What are you called?" but is a polite term we locals use to refer to the rear end, to what bloggers call the arse, to what celebrity buffs refer to as J-Lo's behind, to what rappers call junk in the trunk. You've probably never heard this lyric on the "Baby Got Back" video: "I like big *como se llamas* and I cannot lie." It just doesn't rhyme, no matter how hard you try.

And *pinche* can mean many things, but in the context that had this particular reader perplexed, it meant "tight," "cheap," a penny-pincher, you know, like pinche piker or tight-ass. But that word can also refer to those who are mean or ruthless, or conduct full staff meetings, or, perhaps, if you will, enjoy initiating newcomers to the City Different at Zozobra.

Now I better stop while I'm ahead so that I don't get my own *como se llama* caught up in a sling. Then I'll never be able to run for public office in the event my writing career doesn't work out. Because as Chicano Confucius says, "*Como se llama* follows you 'round rest of life" and "Always be sure to be in front while in crawl space under house, lest *como se llama* in front of you make life unpleasant for a stretch."

But my friend Frank was still confused and he fielded yet another inquisitive question to me. "And *mocosos*—can you translate?"

That, my friend, is what we New Mexicans call our precious little ones and it loosely means "snot-nosed kids." Of course, for all you English-teacher purists out there, the root word of that euphemism is the slang *moco*: "snot" or "booger" to all you fishermen types who should know when it's not cool to slang (or sling) *mocos* (like in the newspaper).

But sometimes the word isn't only used to refer to the little jelly-brained video game players. It's sometimes used to describe certain beginner skiers and snowboarders up at the ski basin. You know the ones, the guys you see from the chair lift walking down the mountain carrying their skis, one glove missing, one pole gone, their jeans and Elmer Fudd caps full of snow, and their faces all *mocoso*. You get my drip, don't ya?

Anyway, to make a long *Animal House* story short, while the Omegas were paddling the crap out of each other's *como se llamas* during their secret initiation rites in one house, the Deltas were partying their *como se llamas* off in another.

Then that *pinche como se llama* Dean Wormer got involved and he wanted to expel those partying Delta *como se llamas* because they were setting a bad example for the mocosos. Anyway, in the end, the Deltas kicked some Omega *como se llama* and our hero Bluto ended up scoring the babe with the finest *como se llama* in the movie.

Oh yeah, and I'm pretty sure that the Kiwanis dudes purposely make Zozobra without one because then he wouldn't be tempted to save his own *como se llama* when he's going up in flames.

Now, aren't we all glad that's behind us?

Remembering That First Glimpse of a White Woman

Sometime ago there was a news report that an airplane flew over a remote section of jungle in South America and a never-known tribe of people was discovered. Reportedly, some of the primitive-living people began firing arrows, spears, darts, and rocks at the low-flying aircraft to ward it off. Of course the whole incident way later turned out to be a hoax, but it didn't stop me from thinking about its implications at the time it happened.

Some anthropologists initially believed that this encounter might have been the first time these remote jungle people had ever been in contact with the outside world. That supposedly new discovery started off a great ethical debate about whether to leave the people alone and let them develop naturally as they were or to contact them—and let them know about the joys of shopping (and more than likely working) at Walmart.

Ironically, just about the time of that news report there was a vintage World War II–era war bird making numerous rumbling, low-flying passes around Santa Fe and the vicinity (including Walmart). Now I don't know if any santafesinos were chucking rocks or sticks or baseballs at the shiny airplane, but it sure was fascinating to watch it in the sky and imagine twenty or more of them flying overhead dropping bombs on the countryside as they were designed to do back in their heyday.

For some reason all this airborne commotion reminded me of a story my dad told me about his growing up on a small ranch in northern New Mexico. Back then, in the 1920s and '30s, "remote" was still a fitting word for this part of state, just the way Don Diego de Vargas begrudgingly described it as "remote beyond compare" when he first encountered New Mexico in his reconquering days of the 1690s. For the common people here before and after the Great Depression, luxuries were few and far between, just as it had been for centuries before that.

Anyway, my dad said that whenever he watched jungle-excursion shows on Channel 5 and he saw all the excited native children running to and surrounding the khaki-wearing safari adventurers, it took him back to the days when he started school in the 1930s. He said there was one particular memory when he and his young elementary-school-age, Spanish-speaking classmates got their first glimpse of an Anglo woman on the playground, who introduced herself to them as their new teacher. Never before had they seen a woman with golden hair and blue eyes so up close and personal and talking to them individually in English, a language still very unfamiliar to them.

All the children, the boys in their denim coveralls and the girls in their best dresses, surrounded her on the playground and looked in awe at their new light-skinned teacher, the likes of whom they had never seen in their village before. My dad says that if there had been a camera recording the action, it could have been a *National Geographic* documentary in its own right on Channel 5.

Just a generation before that, New Mexico still wasn't a state and the people of northern New Mexico were still calling the few Anglos they encountered out in the sticks *americanos* even though technically the norteños were also americanos themselves, whether they knew it or not. If it had been up to the previous generation, people like my father wouldn't have gone to school and they would have stayed working on the ranch every day, just like the many generations before them.

Yep, little did the pint-sized children of that schoolyard in my dad's youth know that they would soon see many more airplanes flying over their heads and many more Anglo schoolteachers in the schoolyard . . . and in the halls . . . and in the stores . . . and on the roads . . . and all around them. They would soon hear many, many more words in English, so many, in fact, that they would teach them to their own children, who in turn would come to know only the English words and not the *palabras* (words) of their ancestors. Then before you know it, out pops a little smart aleck amongst them who would write a cheesy column taking pokes at it all—in English.

I don't know what language that remote tribe in South America spoke, but somehow I just had a feeling that they'd soon be learning the palabras of another culture's language in their not-so-distant future. And when they get their first glimpse of a fair-skinned woman with painted fingernails, painted toenails, and fancy store-bought makeup caked on her face, how will they be able to resist not surrounding her in awe? Kind of sounds like a Tarzan movie, doesn't it, or perhaps *King Kong*? There's no doubt that airplanes have been a major historical disrupter of the natural order. Either they're dropping actual bombs and destroying the countryside, or they're dropping cultural-exchange bombs and influencing the countryside forever.

I'm just grateful that no silvery bombers ever flew over this part of the country to wreak the havoc they've caused in other parts of the world. Luckily, here in New Mexico, the cultural exchange that's dropped from the sky (or off the railroad tracks, or the covered wagons, or the muleskinner's saddlebags, or the bus, or, perhaps, the spaceships) has had so much better impact than TNT.

The more I think of it, cultural exchange is going to be a major dilemma for our newly discovered friends in South America. If and when that happens to them, it's all going to depend on who gets to them first. I guess we can rule out any Chicano expeditions into the Amazon—I gotta go to work in the morning and not gallivanting off into the horizon looking for new species.

And who knows, maybe they'll decide on their own that nail polish and chocolate perfume just aren't for them and au naturel was the better way after all. Nah, I doubt it. Otherwise, our society would have shed our clothes a long time ago.

But one thing I know for sure. They'd never be able to resist green chile!

The Irony Age of New Mexico

One time while I was taking the scenic way back to where I was going, I saw three UPS delivery guys using a cell phone to take pictures of each other in the bright afternoon autumn sunshine on the plaza.

Really no big deal for the most part, until I realized they were taking pictures of each other leaning up against a FedEx delivery van that was parked on San Francisco Street and its driver was nowhere to be seen. Each one of them, clad in the familiar dark-brown uniform of the delivery company, took his turn posing at the back of the van, whose brightly colored FedEx logo stood in brilliant contrast to their own plain but distinctive dress. There they were, three local guys having fun snapping pictures on the plaza, actually behaving in the same manner as the swarms of tourists who surrounded them.

"Hey!" I yelled out my window at them. "The post office is just a couple of blocks that way. You guys should go over there and take some pictures next to the postal service trucks and then you can really say you get around."

They laughed and one of them yelled back at me, "Did you know UPS and FedEx were merging? They're going to call it FedUp!"

Pretty good irony, I thought to myself as I drove away, careful not to hit any of the pedestrians clad in bright flower shirts and Bermuda shorts who had also just taken pictures of themselves next to one of the plain brown stucco walls of La Fonda. They each took turns posing next to the synthetic-finish coating, probably believing it was applied in ancient times. Then they carelessly jaywalked across San Francisco Street, right through the flashing Do Not Walk sign in front of my slow-moving pickup.

That was about the same time another piece of irony smacked me right in the face like a newly bloated property-tax bill that wasn't supposed to increase (at least that was what they told us before the bond elections). We were sitting there at the Capital High football field one windy afternoon waiting for the finish of a YAFL game before my son's team would play.

We sat there watching the Chiefs play the Texans, a team made up of players mostly from the Pecos area and one or two from Las Vegas. The underdog Texans team from Pecos played a tremendous game, and while I watched it, I couldn't believe my ears. Never in my wildest dreams would I ever have imagined a bunch of downtown brown bona fide Chicanos from Pecos passionately cheering on Texans. Every time the young footballers would make a play, the Pecos fans in the stands would yell, "All right, Texans!" or "Let's go, Texans!" or "*Vamanos*, Texans, stop them!"

I hope my history recall isn't playing tricks on me. But during the Civil War, wasn't it a bunch of Texas volunteers in the Confederate Army who were forced out of the Glorieta Pass by a Union regiment of New Mexico volunteers that possibly included some Hispanic infantrymen from the Pecos area?

Pecos could well have been in Texas at one time, because back in the frontier days, Texas in fact claimed that its western border was, indeed, the Río Grande. The Texan government actually sent a tax collector over to New Mexico to gather homage from us New Mexican *pobres*. But the tax collector was promptly tarred and feathered—hopefully not by the people of Pecos, because today some of their descendants are rooting for their own pint-sized version of Texans.

Yep, that's one of the interesting things about irony—it can manifest in some of the most unlikely places. I'm just waiting for the image of the Virgin Mary or even the outline of Christ to appear on the freshly plastered wall of a new American Civil Liberties Union building now that there are plans for the ACLU to expand here in New Mexico. Now that would be irony to light a candle about.

Today, there's even some layered irony occurring within New Mexico's borders. Down south we have this historically dry, 90-mile-or-so stretch of land known as the Jornada del Muerto, or "Journey of the Dead Man" in English. This parched piece of expansive New Mexico soil begins just north of Hatch and ends in the area east of Socorro. It's kind of hard to realize today that the Jornada del Muerto once was one of the most harrowing spans of El Camino Real, especially from the air-conditioned confines of a Subaru wagon or a Chevy truck going 75 mph down I-25. This 1,800-mile-long "Royal Highway," which went from Mexico City north to the Taos area, was the primary thoroughfare of the Spanish and Mexican governments for centuries.

Today, Jornada del Muerto is a rusty irony because New Mexico's largest bodies of water, the man-made Elephant Butte and Caballo Lakes, are situated right dab next to it. Jornada del Muerto is named after a man the Spanish called El Alemán (the German), who died of thirst while traveling through the region. The Spanish accused Bernard

Gruber of practicing witchcraft and he was imprisoned by the Inquisition sometime around 1670. He escaped from Spanish captivity in the Sandía Pueblo District but later died of thirst while on the lam south of Socorro. Thereafter, Herr Gruber's scattered skeletal remains along El Camino Real reminded travelers for many centuries of the tremendous danger of traveling the Jornada del Muerto.

But that's not the only irony of Jornada del Muerto. Officials have located Spaceport America right there in that historically deadly stretch. That's right, 200 grand to take a two-hour flight into the membrane of space, starting right there at good ol' Jornada del Muerto.

I don't know about you, but I don't know what's more scary—taking a commercial ride into space aboard a prototype vessel from an area known as "Journey of the Dead Man" or parting with $200,000. I can just see the promotions now: "Come take a ride into space with us, starting right here in scenic, lovely Jornada del Muerto, known locally as Journey of the Dead Man!"

No thanks. I think I'll just stay on the ground in my trusty burro-powered carreta and save the 200 grand for a down payment on an "affordable" house in south Santa Fe, where the skyrocketing price of real estate is about the closest I'll ever get blasted into space.

The carreta's definitely a lot cheaper and safer. Besides, the bumpy ride lasts a whole lot longer than two hours and the only motion sickness you get is when you're trying to get the stubborn burro into motion. And heck, if the burro refuses to move, I can just sit back, get a tan, and watch the ricos get blasted into the stratosphere.

I'll just make damn sure there's plenty of water for the burro and plenty of cold German beer for me—in honor of El Alemán, the dead man.

There's No Time to Mess Around

A computer guru friend of mine has a favorite techie question he likes to repeat: What's the definition of a computer expert? Answer: Someone who learned how to use a computer six months before you did.

That's pretty funny, but it's been well over six months now that I've learned how to function on a computer and I still find myself running to him every time I have some questions, no matter how dumb. Later on, of course, I realized these questions were pretty dim-witted once he patiently pointed out what I did wrong (like not plugging the mouse into the main hard drive).

The funniest thing he told me about his computer expertise being tapped every six months is the time when a lady came up to him and frantically pleaded that she needed him to come fix her coffee holder.

"What?" he replied. "Computers don't have coffee holders."

He told me he went up to the lady's office and she had been using the retractable CD/DVD tray to hold her coffee mug and it finally gave way to the might and power of Joe, which packed more of a punch than she had realized. My friend made several trips up and down the stairs to help this woman and even after six months she never really became a computer expert compared with the wide-eyed employee they hired just two weeks earlier. It just wasn't in her genes, and I'm assuming that while she was at home, she still had to look at the two-handed clock to see what time it was instead of the blinking VCR.

That proverbial six-month rule got me thinking in general about time-oriented rules, such as the seven-second rule for dropping delectables on the floor and picking them back up to scarf if nobody's looking (except when in a horse stable or the locker room at the Genoveva Chávez Center), or the third-date rule (for all you singles out there who know what I am talking about), or the one-year rule (for widowers ready to get back into the dating game), or the one-minute rule (the time it takes you to slam down this book or search for another story after struggling through the first few paragraphs of one of these cheesy columns).

There are plenty of one-second rules, too, like the time it takes a politician to change his hardened position after some cash is flashed in front of his face (maybe that should change to the nanosecond rule). The one-second rule can also be applied to the time it takes an intuitive woman to decide whether she likes a guy or not, or the time it takes me or any other man to decide if he likes what's on the TV channel before clicking the remote control to the next station. Another one-second rule is the amount of time it takes a typical Santa Fe driver to decide whether to go through the red light or not.

There's also the fifteen-minute rule, or the time it takes you to sit in standstill traffic on I-25 to or from Albuquerque before you decide to hang a U-turn and find the closest alternate route, or the time it takes you to decide whether to wait any longer for the blind date you were supposed to meet at the popcorn stand.

Back in Santa Fe, there are also some ten-second rules, or the time it takes a newcomer or tourist to realize that I'm a true local after opening my accented mouth to give them directions, or the amount of time it takes a local to decide whether to give the correct directions to a newcomer or tourist after they ask which is the fastest way to the "square."

I often wonder if the six-month rule can apply not only to computer experts but also to the length of time someone must live in Santa Fe before they become a local. Or should the "I'm-a-local" rule remain a two-year rule to coincide with the Internal Revenue Service regulations about the length of time you must live in your primary home before you can sell it for profit without tax penalty?

No, maybe not. The two-year rule would probably better be applied to becoming a local entrepreneur—the "flip" rule, for short.

I often christen newcomers as locals, without the so-called required time rules, when they begin using our own hometown jargon. Yes, when I hear my Anglo neighbors call their children *'jita* or *'jito*, then I know they are in the local mindset and it doesn't matter that their newly planted Kentucky bluegrass hasn't begun to turn brown yet.

Or if my new friend from California suddenly starts complaining, "Who in the hell left the gate open?" then I know Old Santa Fe has found a place into his local heart. The left-the-gate-open thing is tricky, however, and must be backed up by accented sayings like "Whazzup, bro?" or, you guessed it, "¡Órale, bro!" for them to be qualified local by me.

You see, "Who left the gate open?" as far as I can tell, is also used by people who call themselves local but whose actions speak otherwise. I often see them on public-access TV lined up in the city council chambers when they find out that a paltry number of affordable homes has been proposed near their golf course and million-dollar homes. Yep, nothing can ruin a good game of golf worse than having to look at regular, hard-working people coming and going from their jobs.

I guess I'm one of those who fit in the lifetime-rule category, or the length of time it takes to live in Santa Fe to be a rooted local. Even though I've lived here more than half a century, I still don't consider myself a Santa Fean. For some odd reason, that term makes me think I'd have to wear custom-made cowboy boots with silver tips, pressed Levis held up by a fancy concha belt capped with a buckle draped in gaudy turquoise, an oversized bolo tie, a suede sport coat, and a cowboy hat. Shakes be to God, I just realized I described J. R. Ewing, and I think he did, indeed, consider himself a Santa Fean, for about two years.

Oh well, I better move along because I'm about to break the twenty-minute rule, or the length of time it takes to read and reread this column to figure out what the heck my point was.

The Fake Tours of Santa Fe

Back in the days when I used to pound the pavement more than I would pound the beers, I was running down a hill near Atalaya Elementary when one of those open buses full of tourists was traveling the other direction.

Without thinking, I decided to have a little fun and just as the bus passed by me, I blurted out one of the most bloodcurdling warrior cries I could muster, using the whole of my rapidly depleting breath. After the bus passed, I heard the tour guide immediately announce through the loud speaker above the laughter of her group, "And yet another example of an indigenous species to Santa Fe, the shrieking bare-chested jogger!"

Every once in a while for fun I'd walk downtown by a group of people following a tour guide and try to listen in to test my own historical knowledge of Santa Fe. Of course, there were many "facts" that came out of some of these tour guides' mouths that I certainly never heard before and certainly will never hear again. Some of these facts went along the lines that the Oldest House was originally built by Aztec Indians to serve as their emperor Montezuma's summer retreat. Or that the plaza was the site of a sacred ancient Indian burial site and the Spanish built the town center over it to spiritually persecute the natives and many believe that the high cost of homes here is the payback for that gesture.

Sure, the facts sounded interesting and sexy enough and the gullible wide-eyed tour goers ate it all up.

But nowadays, before I open up my big trap to let out another warrior shriek to startle a misdirected tour group or, perhaps, a polite and passing "Hogwash" to the tour guide, I usually play it safe and do a little research. I try to be prepared before exposing myself as another species indigenous to Santa Fe, "the whiny, beer-bellied ignoramus."

Nope, I've found no evidence of ancient Aztec civilization in the PERA Building parking lot or along Aztec or Montezuma streets or even at Aztec Optical. And there was no indication of Native American despiritualization near the plaza, other than the disappointed looks on the vendors' faces when various tourists passed on buying a South American windpipes CD near the Loretto Chapel.

It doesn't bother me anymore that an assorted number of visitors go home with a skewed version of Santa Fe history on almost any given day. Rather, it's more important that they finally learn Santa Fe and New Mexico are, indeed, part of the United States and they can safely leave their Visa numbers in our cash registers and their valuable American dollars in the tip jar of their misguided tour guide.

I guess that's a fringe benefit of the tour-guiding business in that one can authoritatively fill in the murky blanks of history while leading an excursion. Hopefully, no one who's along for the ride is a knowledgeable heckler because everyone there might really be in for one interesting trip. But then again there's usually a heckler in every crowd, although a knowledgeable one is another story. Perhaps that's why some of the tour guides I've seen in action around here are able to wing it so regularly.

A friend of mine told me that when he was in college, he and a few of his ornery friends at Fort Lewis College in Durango used to take the guided tour at nearby Mesa Verde National Park. Every time the tour guide would say "Anasazi," they would all reply, "Gesundheit!" No doubt all the other tour goers thought there was something unhealthy being passed around after a few rounds of those antics.

Scholars now frown upon using the word Anasazi, however, and they prefer that others (mainly tour guides and columnists) use the phrase "Ancestral Puebloan" instead to refer to the ancient ones. Linguists claim that "Anasazi" is actually a derivation of a Navajo word that means "enemy of our people" and it's historically inaccurate to use the word to describe the antecedent Pueblo culture.

I think they don't want us to use the word "Anasazi" so that the tour guides at Mesa Verde, Chaco Canyon, Bandelier, and Aztec Ruins don't get heckled so much. In fact, at least one scholar recently claimed there is actual archaeological evidence of cannibalism at Chaco, a theory many vehemently disagree with. But if that turns out to be the case, maybe they'll find out that "Anasazi" really means "tastes like chicken."

And speaking of chicken, another friend of mine told me that they hired a Navajo carpenter to do some work around the house. The carpenter told them that he also used to be a tour guide on a passenger train and he often recounted the story of how Navajos described Kentucky Fried Chicken on the reservation. He told my friend that in the Navajo language there were no words for "finger-lickin' good," so they went around telling each other in Navajo that their KFC meal was "arm-lickin' good." I wonder if the carpenter was pulling my friend's finger, I mean leg, with that story.

Yep, history in the eye of the beholder is also the beauty of Old Santa Fe, where old-timers, newcomers, and visitors alike revel in selectively recounting its past, points of interest, and, most delightfully, idiosyncrasies. Maybe, when my brain finally does dry up, I might get into the tour guide racket and misguide a few souls of my own. I could call my company something like Wayward Tours, or Off the Mark Tours, or Tours at Your Own Risk, or Grain of Salt Tours, or Different City Tours, or Pulling Your Leg Tours, or Mentiroso Map Tours, or . . .

First, I would take my clients to the Eastside and point to a hillside crammed with fancy rico houses. Then I would tell them that my grandpa used to own the whole mountainside but that he lost it all in a craps game at the Camel Rock Casino. Then I would take them by the De Vargas Center mall and I would point out that Don Diego de Vargas forced the natives to build him a shopping center so that they could put a beauty shop there to take care of his long hair.

The plaza is next on the list and I'll point out that scholars actually argue over the official founding date of the city, 1607 or 1609 or 1610.

However, I'll point out that all dates are correct because they actually tried to start construction in 1607 but then the thing got tied up in the historical committee, the planning committee, the archaeological committee, the nonexistent neighborhood committee, and finally the provincial government, which was ordered by the courts three years later to abide by the originally approved plan of 1607.

Man, if this misguided tour-guiding enterprise ever really took off, I know there are plenty of guides out there I could hire who would really fit right in.

Part 3
Canyon Road

I can just imagine a santafesino of the nineteenth century enjoying the solitude of watching his sheep graze under an azure blue sky with puffy clouds lazily floating by when all of a sudden, one, two, three . . . a hundred covered wagons cut across his alfalfa field on their way to the plaza after an adventurous journey from Missouri on the Santa Fe Trail.

Taking the Long Way Is Half the Fun

One night I embarked on a last-minute mission inside Home Depot just before closing time in a futile effort to find a simple plumbing part that, under normal circumstances, I usually trip over on my way to something else. But at the time, the employees were moving nearly everything around as part of an expansion and remodel, and it was a little harder than usual to find anything I was looking for.

During the course of my wanderings, dazed and confused by the new locations of home-repair items whose previous locations I had just became familiar with, I came across my lifelong friend Ben and his wife, Alice, whom I hadn't seen in quite a while. During our youth, I spent many hours in the trenches with Ben. No, we weren't in the military together, but we did spend quite a bit of time alongside each other in the service—in service to his father. Ben and I spent many hours in the trenches with picks and shovels helping his dad, Mr. G, with whatever project he decided to undertake that weekend, utilizing the economical (a fancy word for "free") labor of his sturdy-backed son and gullible friend.

During Mr. G's working years, he went to his high-level government job every workday clad in a suit and tie befitting the big shot that he was. But come quitting time and any other free moment he had on his hands, that suit and tie came off and the worn coveralls went on nearly as fast as a politician forgets your name after he's won the election. In fact, I remember after one of our many trips to the dump, Mr. G, clad in his usual soiled coveralls, decided to make an impromptu stop at a car dealership to take a look-see at the new pickup trucks. He was in the market to replace the one we had just beat up a bit at the landfill.

But, surprisingly, we dusty fellas didn't attract the attention of any salesman at the dealership that day and we wandered the new-car lot without the usual sales-pitch interruptions. After we piled back into Mr. G's beat-up Ford F-150 and made our way back home via Cerrillos Road, I jokingly told him that he should come back some other day in his work clothes—i.e., suit and tie—and maybe a salesman would pay more attention to him.

Working with Ben and his dad in the trenches of their property in Santa Fe, as well as with my own father in the acequias of northern New Mexico, definitely gave me a taste of the hard labor that historically was necessary to settle this rough region that is New Mexico. It also prepared me at a tender age for certain witticisms of construction workers who aspire to be unemployed comedians. For instance, maybe you're there by the garden hose cleaning the boss's tools and suddenly he appears and blurts out at you in front of everyone while he turns off the water, "Whaddya think, you own the water works?!!!"

Then after the token laughter subsides from the rest of the workers, who secretly fear they'll be next in line for a Don Rickles moment, he'll tell the poor hurried young buck cleaning tools to drop everything that just two minutes earlier he was ordered to do and go get him a "left-handed" screwdriver, hammer, or drill, or whatever. And while he's at it, the boss yells, go to the truck and get him his cigarettes, which, of course, the boss forgot on the roof along with the screwdriver, hammer, and drill.

Or let's say the apprentice is hammering some nails and he accidentally bends a nail in half and is struggling to get it out while the boss is watching. No doubt the boss will come over and say, "Son, yah gotta be smarter than the nail."

Boy, I always wish I could see one of these bosses now and teach him some of the other skills that are basically essential to today's world. I'd say stuff like "Hey boss, yah gotta be smarter than the computer" or "Hey boss, you gotta be smarter than the VCR." Or if he walks away and leaves his computer on, I'd tell him, "Whaddya think, you own the Internet?!!!"

Mr. G never insulted us like that, but he did give us some philosophical advice from time to time. One of my all-time favorites to come from his lips: "Don't talk and they won't know you're stupid." I should have listened to him on that one, because throughout the years my smart-aleck ways and big mouth have always alerted people to how stupid I am. I think he offered me that advice one time when he told me to set some bricks in sand through a well-traveled pathway in his backyard. When I told him that I didn't know how to do that, he just laughed and said, "Use your imagination."

Needless to say, that patch of uneven brickwork came out exactly as you'd expect, a shoddy job by an inexperienced fourteen-year-old. It always amazes me that Mr. G never uprooted those bricks and he always made it a point to remind me of them whenever I visited. But now that I have some construction-site savvy behind me, if he had ever brought up my adolescent brick project again, I think I would have told him, "That's okay. I can't see them from my house."

Well, back at Home Depot the loudspeaker is blurting at us to beat-feet it and make our final selections so that the employees can do some more rearranging to confuse us even more on our next visit. That means I have to cut my chat with Ben and Alice short, and while they're walking away, Ben shouts at me, "By the way, I've been enjoying your columns—most of the time!"

"What? Was there one you didn't like?" I asked him curiously, honestly wanting some constructive feedback.

"Well, sometimes you get going on something and then you go off somewhere else," he said as he walked away. "Then you have to read it again to get your point."

Boy, did that jettison me back to Earth in a flash. After he was gone, I realized that maybe I write like I shop at Home Depot. I go into the store looking for a simple plumbing part. Then I get sidetracked by some interesting stuff on another aisle. Eventually, I end up leaving the store without my plumbing part, but I have $65 worth of other things that I never intended to buy.

I guess that does sound sort of like these columns. Oh well, what the heck! I don't have to read it at my house.

Piece by Piece It All Comes Together

I'll be the first to admit that there's quite of lot of mystery involved in being a writer. That obscure area of the mind where ideas come from isn't always easy to describe. That's why a lot of times you see us egghead writer types at work with our feet propped up on the desk and staring out the window with a faraway look in our eyes, searching for inspiration.

That's also the reason you won't see too many writer types working the front counter at the Motor Vehicles field office, or as a teller in a bank on busy payday Friday, or as a cashier at the local grocery store where only one register is open during coupon happy hour.

You also won't see too many scribes working in the construction industry either, because a foreman will take one look at a writer seeking inspiration under a shade tree, looking up at the puffy clouds during a concrete pour, and then send the thoughtful fella home with a bruise on his *como se llama* from a well-placed, steel-toed work boot.

But in all reality, writers can be hard to spot in a crowd, that is, if they're not working in a job where most eyes in the room are upon them and there's an impatient customer in line complaining that proper procedure isn't being followed because the idiot on the other side of the counter keeps meandering off into the ozone.

Writers come in all shapes and sizes, and the only thing that is more varied than their packaging is the source of their ideas, which basically come from—drumroll, please—who in the heck knows where?

Sometimes, I just can't help but think that the idea well is much like the unseen aquifer: you can only draw from it for a certain length of time before it has to be recharged again. Otherwise, you really have to dig deeper and deeper to find what you're looking for.

In my case, I compare the accumulation of ideas for a story with a general handyman, one of those resourceful types who saves every little screw, washer, spring, oddly shaped plastic fitting, spark plug, piece of hose, doorknob, cabinet handle, flashlight bulb, rubber band, pocket knife, nail, wire, bracket, and whatever else might come in handy in the future.

And you can tell a handyman who's on the ball because in his workshop he has all of these little knickknacks organized into glass jars and buckets, sliding trays and racks, hooks and rafters, behind workbenches and other hidden stash places where only he can find them. In fact, on the back of this handyman's little beat-up pickup with a black utility rack and silver toolbox there's a bumper sticker that reads "Save Your Nuts and Bolt."

You see, sometimes writers have this smorgasbord of random ideas that they stash in the far corners of their minds, ready to be retrieved in a pinch. Just like the handyman's stash of doohickeys: one by itself isn't really worth anything, but when it fits in perfectly as a piece of the puzzle, it's as good as gold. Because who wants to drive all the way down Cerrillos Road to Big Jo's to buy a little piece of $#!+ part that you threw away just last week because you got tired of seeing it around for years and thought you'd never need it in a million years?

So that's why when you read these writings, sometimes they seem a little nuts and every once in a while you feel like you've been screwed (especially when the vending machine took your money and you had to put another fifty cents in to get a paper).

Or maybe something was missing and just one little piece, a scrap nail perhaps, could have held it all together or, maybe, made it make a little more sense. But honestly, sometimes after cooking up a cheesy column, you end up with more spare parts than you started with, just like the kid's new bicycle on Christmas morning.

When that happens, sometimes I have a hard time realizing there are other choices than going out and getting hammered. Who cares if someone took one of these creations apart with their own stash of literary chisels? There's always a new project down the line and the public has a short memory, because in this business it's always about "What have you done for me lately?"

Okay, a well-thought-out story line is the best way to go, and if you want a solid structure, you shouldn't be using spare parts and scraps anyway. But when that writing deadline comes roaring down the track like a runaway locomotive and there's little time to save yourself much less the children, those salvaged ideas come in pretty handy. Especially when the library is closed, the Internet's down, it's been a slow news week, or the kids haven't done something so terribly darling lately that I felt I just had to share it with the rest of the world.

So there you have it. I've essentially just admitted that I'm a scrappy writer, just like that short scrappy basketball player who seems to come up with the loose ball amongst the trees, in the paint or that short-order cook who'll complete the meal to the delight of an unknowing customer even though it's really not quite what the menu promised.

Yep, whenever I get around to writing my epic novel, it won't be *War and Peace*, it'll probably be *War and Pieces*. It won't be *Ben-Hur*, it'll be *Bien-Blur*. Or maybe it could be based on that historic village formerly known as San Juan Pueblo and I'll call it *I'm Ohkay, You're Ohkay*.

But enough malarkey, let's get back to that shed full of salvaged hardware and ideas, also known at my casa as the doghouse. And believe you me, with a pair of loose-fitting smarty pants like mine, I'm always in there looking for something. In fact, I was in there just the other day looking for some leftover ideas from the last story that would have securely tied this piece together so that I wouldn't have to go to the light-bulb store at the eleventh hour.

Now if only I could have remembered where I put them, I might have nailed it.

Is There a Cliché in the House?

There are some things that are just too gosh-darn hard to admit. Plain and simple. A tough pill to swallow. A *chile relleno* too spicy to bite. A dirt road too bumpy to ride. A river too dry to drink. A mountain too private to climb. A woman too beautiful to approach.

Well, before some of you start thinking that I'm about to spill my guts all over this column or shed a crocodile tear over spilled milk, I'll try not to beat around the bush. I once saw an old teacher of mine and she pointed out to me that somewhere out there was an educator in front of a pack of wide-eyed, frothing-at-the-mouth high school students who had been using a column or two of mine as part of their English lessons.

Talk about sending a chill up my spine, I felt like I was going down Jack's Creek without a paddle. It was enough to make a grown man cry, but I knew that the teachers had to keep the wheel spinning so that these kids wet behind the ears hopefully would grow into fine upstanding citizens, meaningful contributors to society, pillars of the community.

The last time something churned in my stomach like this was way back when, once upon a time when I heard my old college journalism professor was using the school's student newspaper (of which I was editor at the time) as an example of what *not* to do in general journalism.

Of course, a couple of years earlier when I was in his classroom trying to learn the ropes, little did I know he would later have me on the ropes, but I wasn't there to take one on the chin, let alone take a dive. This professor would make a habit of devoting his whole class sessions to the local papers, tearing them to bits and pieces, just like the paper shredders create the innards of Zozobra every year just to go up in ashes to the delight of the madding crowd.

Before that, the only newspaper I ever saw getting torn to shreds was in my carefree years when I was about yea high, you know, knee-high to a grasshopper. I used to own a large pet rat against my mother's wishes that I named Herman, and I kept that critter in a cage in my room. It didn't take long for Herman's freshly cleaned, newspaper-lined cage to look like it got in a catfight and, of course, smell like an evening in Paris to boot. Talk about an introduction to yellow journalism.

But the thing that I remember the most about that ol' journalism professor's lessons was the time he spent a whole hour talking about the use of those dastardly clichés. You know, the squeaky wheel gets the grease, the meowing kitty gets the milk, the early bird gets the worm, the cheesy column gets the outhouse.

Ever since that fateful day when he impressed upon us to avoid the use of the dreaded cliché at all costs, I felt like it was time to call it a day, turn in my keys, turn the other cheek, howl at the moon. Because before then, the use of a cliché or two was my writing lifeline (not to mention my personality) and forbidding that was like taking a bone away from a dog, heading into the eye of the storm, throwing in the towel. Yep, after that day I felt like life suddenly became a dark and stormy night and it was time to take shelter from the storm.

With the use of clichés, I always thought the future looked bright, I could ride into the sunset, aim for the stars. But without them, I would be like a moth drawn to the flame, a cowboy without a horse, a rebel without a cause, a Laurel without a Hardy, a Lucy without a Ricky.

This professor was telling us the unthinkable, sending us budding journalists into the cruel, harsh world without a pun, like going into gunfight without a gun, or a model into a photo shoot without makeup. Now that was something to shake a stick at, a pill hard to swallow I mean, and I wasn't going to go down without a fight. He could have my clichés when he pried them from my cold dead fingers. But deep down I knew I was fighting a losing clause, I mean cause, like, like the kid who complains that eating leftovers is like eating "used food" but he eventually succumbs to the gurgles of hunger and eats his own words as well as the dried up potatoes, which didn't taste so bad after all drowned in ketchup.

So now, as far is writing is concerned, I know not to go down that familiar road, that it's best to go down the path less traveled. Take the high road, not the dirt road, and realize that every dog will have its day and it's best to let sleeping dogs lie.

I heard my once insightful professor is retired now, out to pasture to smell the roses with all the other educators turned out to stud with their mimeograph machines, whose freshly pressed copies' smell could put any dreamy-headed student's mind in the clouds. The late comedian George Carlin often remembered the time when his teacher told him to write a paper in his own words. Of course, Carlin found this a daunting task because he said he always spoke and wrote with the words everybody else was using—namely, English.

So at the risk of not repeating myself, I'm resting assured that the kids are out of school for the summer and the teachers are also away from their classrooms doing whatever teachers do in the summer. And, hopefully, this piece of work will never make it into the do's and don'ts of correct English, or even Spanglish for that matter, and it doesn't end up shot full of holes and riddled with bullets of critique, gunned down like a dog in broad daylight!

But to cliché or not to cliché, that is the question, and unfortunately, it does not take a holiday. But, hopefully, many of our sprouting young writers can nip that cliché dilemma in the bud and not repeat the mistakes of the past and yearn for what the future will bring. But I'm sure they'll cross that bridge when they come to it and figure it will all come out in the wash.

And now that this piece is done, I can go fry bigger fish and then go back to sleep and all the rest.

When You Have to Use Your Own Words

At one time there was a very friendly maintenance man who routinely took care of the old building where I worked during the day. This historic state building, which was originally built in the 1880s as part of St. Michael's College, was eventually named after Governor Lew Wallace, who was sent to New Mexico to repair quite a few messes, both in the southern and northern parts of the state.

You might know Wallace as the pen pal of our own beloved Billy the Kid, or maybe as the author of the epic novel *Ben-Hur: A Tale of the Christ*. This Territorial Era governor is also famous among us pessimists for being credited with that infamous evaluation of our great state, "Every calculation based on experience elsewhere fails in New Mexico." I guess that line alone makes it one of our state's great ironies that a building dedicated to Wallace always seems to have so many things going wrong with it.

Yes, our beloved maintenance man was always running from one end of the building to the other or climbing on top of the roof or descending into the basement. He was either fixing someone else's fix or creating a new fix that, eventually, also had to be fixed. And if he wasn't tinkering on a repair, he was running up and down the stairs to the boiler room because the puffy-cheeked office workers were complaining it was too cold in the morning, then too hot when the sun came out in the afternoon. (In the summertime, these same pasty-faced workers complained it was too hot in the morning and then too cold by the afternoon when the air conditioning got going.)

This poor maintenance man could never win, but I swear he tried harder than anyone I ever saw, before or after, in his position. When it rained, he was up on the roof patching one of the many leaks that had made its way into the interior ceiling, and when it snowed, he was making the rounds, making sure the windows were sealed and the icy sidewalks were clear so that none of the wobbly-walking workers fell on their behind or their puffy cheeks.

Every time you'd hear an unearthly squeal come from one of the offices, shortly afterward there he was with a mousetrap or some other type of funky device designed to capture the little critters that made natural sopranos out of more than one of us. (Before some of you start snickering, when I walk into a room, the mice jump on chairs, to coin an old phrase.) Although our maintenance guy was usually on the ball, one day I heard him complaining while he was fixing a leaky heating pipe in the ceiling that had dripped hot water onto one of the computers during the night.

"I don't know what they expect me to do," he said in a frustrated voice while shaking his oil-stained finger in the air. "All of these things break down in this building and they don't give me any materials to fix them. Then I have to go take care of another building and it's the same thing over there. I always have to use my own tools from home."

I have to admit I felt sorry for the guy. He used to own his own construction company and he knew what it took to get a job done. But in his maintenance position at the Lew Wallace Building, improvisation was the word of the day, five days a week. I started thinking about what he said about having to bring his own tools from home and I thought to myself, "Hell, I'm in the same boat!" The editors at Journal North expect me to write a column every two weeks and "I always have to use my own words from home." So I figured that maybe I should start thinking about column-writing the way a construction dude thinks about a project.

First, I'll demand half of the money up front for materials. In this case the materials are my words, and they ain't cheap. Talk is cheap, but my words aren't, even if I buy them wholesale down at the Word Depot (that's the library to most of you folks). The editors tell me they want a column with a lot of anecdotes and maybe a metaphor here or there. Well, I'll pull out my notebook, jot down a few illegible notes, and point out to them that I can use plenty of anecdotes off the shelf but the original ones are considered custom and I'll have to get more money up front for them.

And metaphors, well, those are special order and they're on back order most of the time. Just because I like them, I'll give them a good deal on an expensive allegory that I had left over from a job I did for some ricos in Las Campanas, but they probably won't go for that because there's not enough square-footage in this column. I'll tell them that clichés are the cheapest way to go and there are plenty of cliché kits off the rack that I could use to slap a column together in no time. Such kits are bountiful on the Internet and all you have to do is possess semiadequate skills at another tool (or dirty little secret) of the scribe trade: the copy-and-paste functions in your software.

Oh my! This column is due and I haven't even started it yet. Man, I knew I shouldn't have used all of those anecdotes and metaphors that the *Journal North* paid for on that other story I've been working on. I should have saved a few of them. Oh well, thank God for the Internet. What?!!! My Internet's down!

Oh-oh! The phone's ringing and the caller ID's showing that it's the editor from the *Journal North*. He's probably calling about this column, which was due yesterday at the meeting I didn't show up to. I'll let the answering service pick up. Man, am I slick or what?

Well, on second thought I better not approach column-writing like a construction dude. I'll just take a cue from my friend the maintenance worker, even if it does mean I'll have to "use my own words from home."

Change Is Constant in Same Ol' Santa Fe

The earliest I can consciously remember Santa Fe actually physically changing was during the mid-1970s. The city had undergone many lasting major alterations just a few years earlier, during the federally funded urban-renewal craze that swept the nation during the 1960s. The urban-renewal fervor was probably the last time most of the Santa Fe townsfolk willingly and wholeheartedly approved of the condemnation and demolition of many buildings that now, arguably, could be considered historic. Of course when I say "most," I'm talking about the people who weren't getting their own property condemned in the process.

Such renewal and revitalization meant that many longtime homes and structures were condemned and people were forced to move away from locations that their families had lived in for generations. If not for such actions, many locations in Santa Fe that have become essential icons wouldn't be here today. I can't imagine twenty-first-century life without the State Capitol "Roundhouse," St. Francis Drive, Guadalupe Street, Paseo de Peralta, or Chicago Dog. I can just see the traffic jams in crowded Santa Fe today if urban renewal had never occurred. It probably would be like having the drivers of hundreds of cars on both sides of the northern village of Córdova all attempting to get to the other side of the community at the same time. No doubt this is a seemingly impossible task, even for two hungry herds of cattle late for feeding time in opposite fields.

That urban renewal and the forced relinquishing of property is in dramatic contrast to today's prosperous Santa Fe, where so many wholeheartedly sell, ending the multigenerational family connection to their homes and neighborhoods even without a major thoroughfare involved. Families who had their homes condemned back then will attest to the measly amounts offered by the city.

Most of this major urban renewal occurred while I was still a gradeschooler and oblivious to the bulldozers rumbling around me. Back then I was more concerned about making my way down to the pinball and vending machines inside the Coronado Lanes bowling alley on Cordova Road than realizing the unfortunate plight of some of my fellow santafesinos. Or if our childhood pockets were empty on any given day, we'd spend the afternoon catching tadpoles and frogs at a small pond that used to sit on the northwestern outskirts of what is now known as Salvador Perez Park. There haven't been wild frogs for years in Santa Fe. Burgeoning populations of prairie dogs have symbolically replaced them in our parks.

An Australian speculator once moved into our neighborhood for a brief period, and I kept a cautious eye out for those pesky cane toads that were introduced into his country to control a beetle problem before they proliferated out of control. Who knows, a cane toad egg might have made it across the ocean on the sole of his shoe and it might've grown into an adult and hopped from his place into mine. It could be a signal of a riveting, or shall I say "ribbitting," resurgence of the croaked Santa Fe frogs of my youth that never benefited from the legal protection prairie dogs now enjoy.

No doubt the urban-renewal efforts of the 1960s left many people scarred when their properties were taken away from them through eminent domain. Some of these unfortunate residents let it be known that they were still smarting from these backhoe wounds when Debbie Jaramillo became mayor. Jaramillo often brought up these condemnations when there were demands, as there still are, to extend Richards Avenue from Rodeo Road to West Alameda, which was also on the table at the time to be widened to relieve traffic congestion. Obviously, there are a lot of homes in this path that the Richards Avenue crow flies. Now that they've extended Siler Road across the Santa Fe River to West Alameda to relieve traffic, many stories of the 1960s condemnations have been resurrected, as they should be, for they are part of our local history, which literally involves many centuries of growing pains.

I can just imagine a santafesino of the nineteenth century enjoying the solitude of watching his sheep graze under an azure blue sky with puffy clouds lazily floating by, when all of a sudden, one, two, three . . . a hundred covered wagons cut across his alfalfa field on their way to the plaza after an adventurous journey from Missouri on the Santa Fe Trail. People always will find shortcuts wherever possible and the unfortunate ones along the crow's path historically have had to suffer the consequences. A friend of mine who used to live along a moderately quiet Northside street woke up one day and found himself routinely yelling at the sudden onslaught of speeding motorists when a housing development sprouted nearby. His street abruptly became the quickest way to the plaza from this new development and he had to resort to what he called "Chicano speed bumps" because of a lack of foresight and traffic enforcement from the city.

What are these, you ask? Well, he went down to the nearest arroyo and found some of the biggest boulders he could handle on his own and he randomly placed them along the side of the street so that the speeding cars had no choice but to slow down and, of course, they were too rushed to get to the plaza to get out of their cars to move the boulders out of their way for the return trip. My friend eventually moved, and the Chicano speed bumps were replaced by "traffic control" mounds (a fancy lawsuit-prevention word).

Eminent domain and condemnation are, indeed, thorny subjects. Just ask the US Supreme Court, which ruled it lawful to utilize eminent domain for private development. Public outcry over this outrageous ruling reverberated in the halls of Congress. At least one candidate for mayor once promised, if elected, that an official city resolution outlawing this type of eminent domain in Santa Fe would occur if he was elected. Before the city closes the book on condemnations, however, perhaps there are a few things they could do beforehand.

Maybe the city could condemn Frenchy's Field and make a real park out of it, instead of forcing the children in that area to be driven across town to play with a ball without getting an unwelcome dose of *palitos* (splinters). And while they're at it, maybe they could condemn the "award-winning" El Zocalo on the city's hilly Northside and give it a paint job so that it at least looks like it belongs there.

And if the city was really in a Wednesday-night, eminent-domain mood, it also could condemn the Eldorado Hotel and let them put the Super Walmart in there instead of on the Southside. It's already an existing big box and, besides, it would get more locals back into the downtown area—as long as Walmart gave them parking validations. And, on the bright side, now that there's a ban on plastic shopping bags in the city, we wouldn't even see those blue plastic Walmart bags blowing out of control on the plaza, and, to boot, there wouldn't be any more bottles being thrown off the balconies during out-of-control Susanami pizza parties.

Okay, I admit I'm losing sight of the crow's path here, but I seriously do wish the city would condemn Siberian elms. Someone brought them here way back when to remedy our lack of shade, and look what happened! They've leapfrogged into the New Mexican version of the cane toad and are creating Chicano rainforests as far as the eye can see!

And, by the way, my Australian friend leapfrogged outta my neighborhood once he flipped his house and the illegal condo he plopped in the back.

Down in the Dumps at Christmas

I remember one Christmas season when I admit I was a little down in the dumps. But the way I was down in the dumps was really different from the way I used to really get down in the dumps. The real reason behind my "holiday" dilemma was that local officials had just announced that we Santa Fe–area regular residents could no longer take our truckloads of rubbish to the Caja del Rio Landfill facility. After that 2006 New Year, we all had to make the trip back to the old dumping grounds overlooking the city off Paseo de Vista because some dump novice in a Saab parked his car to unload behind a moving, working bulldozer. Need I say more?

I admit that it was definitely a bummer for regular dump users like me when the new transfer station opened up at the old dump in the 1990s. For all of our lives up until that point, going to the dump was free, frolicky, and happy-go-lucky. There was always plenty of seemingly cool stuff you'd see just lying around begging you to take it home. I don't know how many times I thought I spotted something shiny, and therefore valuable, in the trash heap next to me. Before you knew it, this new collectible, which I thought I could fix or "use somewhere for something because it just looked like it," was in the bed of my pickup and heading back home with me.

I'm sure there are more locals out there with their own similar landfill stories where a newfound "valuable" made the roundtrip from the dump, to the house, and then back to the dump again a few weeks—or a few years—later because it turned out not to be so valuable after all. Either that or the wife gave it one of those looks and then it wasn't so cool anymore.

The new transfer station changed all of that. New rules, which are still in place today, prohibited such handyman bargain hunting at the dump. And not only that, there were now limited hours for dumping, you had to cover your trash loads or face a fine, you had to show them your driver's license, and, probably the most difficult to swallow of them all, you had to *pay* to do your dumping.

No longer was it the happy dumping grounds of my youth, when, for twenty-four hours a day, seven days a week, we locals were in dump heaven. Every new trip to the old dump offered a new adventure where the heavy-equipment operators bladed new roads to fresh dumping grounds that sometimes could be as much as fifty feet deep (more or less) from the surface of the piñon, juniper, and soiled-mattress-and-sofa-studded hills.

When the transfer station opened, all of a sudden the law-laden rules of the rest of the world hit us like a dump truck. Now we had to know the hours of the dump, which are never enough for a long summer day, we had to have plenty of cash on hand to leave our load, and we had to hand over our driver's license so that they knew exactly who we were. The freedom of the old dump was buried forever along with the trash loads of our ancestors.

It took me a long time to get used to this new aspect of Santa Fe that never in a million years I thought would occur. It was now more expensive to go to the dump than it was to play a round of golf. First they wanted $15, then they weighed your truck, and then they directed you inside the transfer station. Now that I think of it, the inside of the transfer station is about as big box as Walmart and most of the stuff in there looked like it came from that store, minus the fancy packaging that most likely arrived there in a black trash bag many months before.

In the past, we'd hurl our loads from the truck to the dirt or other trash heaps at the old open-air dump. But inside the transfer station it all falls onto sloped concrete where it is shoved by a huge front-end loader into a semitrailer destined for the Caja del Rio Landfill. And boy, if you see a ball or an end table that looks like it still has a little life left in it on that concrete pad, you better not even think of picking it up for a twenty-first-century roundtrip to your house. If the fast-moving front-end loader doesn't get you trying to make your impromptu salvage, one of the dump employees will get you—with a citation for illegal scavenging.

On my first trip to the transfer station checkpoint, they said I owed $39 for my new dumping experience. "What?!!!" My load consisted of green leaves, branches, and wood stumps from that pesky Siberian elm weed, I mean tree, that I finally chopped down. I got tired of it cracking my wall, wreaking havoc on the sidewalk, clogging the sewer lines every growing season, and, most of all, sharing its unholy, unwanted seed throughout the whole neighborhood. In my mind, I thought I was performing a community service getting rid of that organic nuisance, but instead I had to fork over my week's Lotaburger money and my reserve funds for a six-pack and some delicious Posa's tamales. I got a double dose of the modern world's reality the day I began to learn the new idiosyncrasies of Santa Fe dump dynamics.

In the beginning, the pleasant and highly courteous dump people— at least they started out that way—made you pay in cash or let you write a check. They didn't take credit cards. Eventually, I guess they got tired of accepting bad checks that had more business inside the trash than in their checkpoint cash register. And if you didn't like the new rules or didn't have enough cash on hand at that moment, an AKAL security guard was ready to follow you so that your load didn't miraculously disappear into one of the nearby arroyos.

That's when I discovered the Caja del Rio Landfill. It was a breath of fresh air, where for $5 you could dump a covered pickup-bed-level load out in the great outdoors just like the good ol' days. And they let you pay just $3 if you had to unload a green load of community-service work (filleted Siberian elm trees) or bark-beetle-infested piñon trees.

When they closed our public access to Caja del Rio, we all had to go through the "dump learning curve" at the transfer station all over again. That's why I was so down in the dumps that one Christmas. I had to figure out how much it was going to cost me to get rid of all of last year's Christmas heap to make room in the house for the next year's Walmart pile. Bah dumpbug!

To Be Local, You Must First Get Off

I received an interesting email from a woman who told me these "¡Órale!" columns are a hoot to her but that her husband "just doesn't get it."

Of course, I must point out that the gracious lady wrote that she was born and raised in Santa Fe but her husband grew up out of state and often doesn't understand the local witticisms that so many northern New Mexicans have been exchanging all their lives. The more she tried to explain local traditions and mannerisms, the more he just scratched his head in confusion.

I felt sorry for the poor lad, you know, because marriage is hard enough without having to learn a whole new set of ingrained values, traditions, and culture (a group of nice words for historical idiosyncrasies). Add to this man's perplexity my own twisted take on our unique existence here and I'm sure this guy is really wondering what the heck he got himself into when he said, "I do."

I'm sure this local woman has already "trained" her man to expect that posole and red chile are as much a part of Thanksgiving and Christmas around here as the turkey and Christmas tree. And I'm sure he learned all by himself to never, ever, ever earnestly refer to a farolito as a luminaria during the holidays or risk the northern New Mexican equivalent of a tar and feathering—downing a generous shot of cheap tequila chased by an explosive jalapeño that must be chewed and swallowed whole lest he face the wrath of another.

I'm sure by now this fellow realizes that he *must* look both ways before crossing the street anywhere downtown because despite what he learned about Santa Fe on the other side of the continent, those are real cars and not burros. And if this guy ever comes close to being like the rest of us, he's going to instinctively drive south instead of east when he wants to buy groceries or a pair of jeans or a tank of gas. On the other hand, when his kin visit from out of state, he's going to instinctively drive east instead of south for a more refined tour of the city.

Our former mayor Debbie Jaramillo once (or was it several times?) referred to the newcomers of our city as "just off the bus." I think she had this wrong. Gauging by the prices many of our newly arrived Santa Feans are paying for these incredible new homes that are light-years away from my own pocketbook, I seriously doubt they just got off the bus. I think more realistically they just "emerged from the Mercedes" or maybe they "popped out of the Lear."

In my own case, they tell me I arrived "just off the gurney" at the old Marion Hall birthing section at St. Vincent's Hospital off Palace Avenue. A friend of mine who also happens to be an archivist researched the

Vigil family tree and learned my paternal ancestors arrived "just off the carreta" from Zacatecas, Mexico, with Don Diego de Vargas during the Spanish reconquest in 1693.

Don't get me wrong. Not all Santa Feans have emerged from expensive SUVs, exploded from the womb, or endured a thousand-mile carreta ride from Mexico during colonial times. Some long-haired Santa Feans arrived in the 1960s "just off the VW bus" while others in the 1800s first came "just off the covered wagon" or, later, "just off the Super Chief."

I'm sure there are some people who live here now who first arrived when hitchhiking. To these hardy souls, I say you arrived "just off the pavement." Honestly, it's really hard to generalize how people came here, but I'm going to go out on a limb and say that I don't think anybody came "just off the boat," unless, of course, it was being pulled on a trailer.

Of course, there are new arrivals we never see because they spend most of their time behind high adobe walls and gated communities, and when they finally do emerge and look down on our Santa Fe service community, you know they arrived "just off their high horse." And if the inspired souls in Roswell are right in believing that there really are extraterrestrials wandering among us, you can bet this stealthy group of characters certainly arrived here "just off the flying saucer."

All right, before I start getting more and more "off the point," I'm sure that when this local lady's husband now goes back to his hometown to visit, some of his townsfolk tell him that he now talks with an accent even though he doesn't think so. Never mind that he now routinely yells out of his car at the tourists walking in the middle of the road near the plaza to "get off the way." That sort of thing tends to happen when some newcomers take the time to morph into santafesinos, usually by osmosis. First thing you know, they're going "*ah la*," "*eeeee!*" "Hey, bro!" or "pinche this" or "pinche that."

And just about the same time a *ristra* appears on their porch, they start complaining that somebody "left the gate open," because so many more are arriving here "just off of something or another" and those strangers are calling the candlelit bags "luminarias," to add insult to injury.

I don't know if this nice local lady ever showed this particular piece to her husband because I'm pretty sure he probably "won't get it" again, especially with all the exaggerations and malarkey and all.

I'd be personally satisfied if she handed him this writing and he retorted, "Oh sí, snap!" On the other hand, maybe he'll read it and subconsciously declare, "Oh yeah, know?"

Now that would be something to get off on.

Keep Supply of Snappy Comebacks Handy

Just a handful of years ago (actually it literally was more like the last century) a group of us local aging basketball players used to rent out the Santa Fe Prep gym for about an hour or so every week in an attempt to relive our glory days on the court.

We would each contribute $4 and rent the gym from the private school for an hour of gasping, hacking, and ankle-rolling fun with an occasional swish thrown in here and there. Afterward, some of us would waddle out of the gym like Fred Sanford over to one of the guy's house for some beers and grub and continue to relive the slow-motion action that had just occurred earlier in the night. If we were lucky enough to get through that brutal sixty minutes of full-court action in one piece, we could spend several more hours going through it again and again, only more spectacular the second and third time around through our beer goggles.

This had been going on like clockwork for nearly every Monday night for several years whether it was raining or snowing or sunny or dark outside. One night I walked in the gym a little late and a guy named Ted excitedly came up to me—at least he made it seem that way—and he declared, "Arnold, I'm sure glad you showed up!"

"Really, why?" I replied to him, proudly thinking to myself that he was happy to see my three-inch vertical jump shot finally arrive to help out his team.

"Because now I'm not the fattest guy here!" he cracked.

Okay, he got me, and I can just hear some of you snickering too. But after the chuckles died down, we got down to some old-fogey basketball and I might have paid him back with a well-placed hack or two, but that's something that any seasoned has-been hoopster will never admit to. Besides, ol' Ted supplied me with a versatile line that I continue to use today, more times than not with a different adjective inserted to suit whatever situation might arise.

It's smart to have a good supply of such comebacks because you never know when you're going to need them. Like the time I was skiing with a buddy of mine named Rick up at Taos Ski Valley. After waiting in line a good fifteen minutes or so to get on the chair lift, it was finally our time to get on a swift-moving chair.

"Heavier skiers, please sit on the left side of the chair," the lift operator told us two husky fellas.

"Arnold, you better get to the left!" Rick immediately replied, beating me to the punch line and getting the laughter of all around within earshot, especially the two grade-school-age kids behind us, who seemed to be having their own little verbal rivalry going as well.

"Yeah, you're right, Rick," I replied loudly back at him, my mind racing a million miles a second searching for a least some type of honorable response. "Muscle weighs more than fat!"

Right then we both slid onto the loading point, the chair swiftly swooshed us away, and we could hear the crowd behind us whooping. But best of all, Rick had no chance for a comeback and we finished our ride to the top of the mountain with myself the slimmer of the two, at least when I stood next to him.

Meanwhile, one wintry night back at the prep school gym, a younger guy, probably in his early to mid twenties and clad in a Dallas Cowboys sweatshirt, walked in and declared that he'd heard up at the ski basin where he worked that there was some pickup basketball being played there on Monday nights.

"Yeah, you can play," someone replied, "but you're going to have to leave that Cowboys shirt outside!" After a smattering of chuckles here and there—it wasn't unanimous because most of the players were Cowboys fans—we all learned that this fella was indeed from the revered city of Dallas itself.

Boy, I'm telling you, he never should have admitted that. I made tears well up in this guy's eyes one time when I asked him if he wanted some more Cowboys garb, which I could get him for free.

"Yes!" he exclaimed, obviously excited to get some gear from his favorite team.

"Okay," I told him. "I see it at the dump all the time. I'll start getting it for you."

"How can you say that?" he replied back, obviously upset that someone would dare razz him about his favorite team. He quickly learned that no professional team was sacred in those pickup basketball games and the more you defended your team preference, the more ribbing you could expect to receive.

This friendly Texan once told me that his brother was going to be visiting Santa Fe and he warned his sibling to never, ever bring up the subject of the Alamo when he was around us because that was a very touchy subject. I had to inform him that besides the history books, the only Alamo we ever really knew around here was the street we took to get to the old dump. But we did get really passionate about it at one time—that was when they put speed bumps all along it, so it made our heavy pickup loads bounce more than they should, especially when you were trying to get to the dump before closing time.

Yes, we were quite the tricultural bunch—Hispanics, Anglos, and Texans—at those preppy pickup basketball games on Monday night, and we all got along famously. In fact when it came time for us to each ante up the $4 every time to pay the piper, no one seemed to mind when I would yell out in the thickest Spanish accent I could muster, "¡Quatro pesos y los gringos DIEZ!" (Four dollars and the Anglos ten!)

After a couple years of these antics, my Lone Star friend had finally had enough when he exclaimed back in his own thick Texan accent, $4 in hand, "How long do I gotta live here before I ain't no gringo no more?!!!"

Of course, I had to tell him that people have been pondering that question in Santa Fe for centuries.

Mysteries along the Dirt Road

Sometimes it seems as if more and more streetlights pop up by the day and more and more businesses stay open later through the night. Are the mystique and wonderment of Santa Fe (and northern New Mexico for that matter) slowly but surely being eroded by the advances of our modern world?

Many will contend that the advent of technology has little to do with the City Different becoming ever so bland. Rather, they will argue that the noticeable changes can be attributed to the massive influx of people, wealth, and new ideas that have permeated our city for the past thirty or forty years.

There is no doubt that a group of children from the past, walking home from a school dance down a winding dirt road with nothing but the stars and the moon to light their way and casting roadside shadows to tantalize their imaginations, will draw upon some sort of mystery and intrigue to occupy the passing conversation.

On the other hand, fast-forward to today and place this same group of children in an SUV driven by a soccer mom who humors the kids by playing their favorite rap-music station as she drives each of them home. Suddenly the mystery and intrigue of the world is not quite the same, other than the puzzle of why the radio went silent for about ten seconds and the DJ later announced his programming blunder but didn't offer details.

It seems that we don't pay attention to mystery and intrigue as much today, especially when the television and stereo are blaring and children and adults alike must raise their voices in order to be heard. Or maybe it's because we fail to notice life passing us by as we go through our daily routines in a daze, like the soccer mom who methodically takes all the youngsters home so that they can be united once again with their iPods and PlayStations.

Don't get me wrong. There are still plenty of pockets of mystique and intrigue throughout Santa Fe and you're still going to find them in pretty much the same places they've always been. Take for instance the

"Miraculous Stairway" in the Loretto Chapel. Throughout my lifetime and others' stretching back to the late 1800s, many of us believed that a mysterious unknown carpenter created the masterpiece whose identity we wholeheartedly and faithfully attributed to St. Joseph. Now, through the indefatigable efforts of one local historian, one of our most cherished Santa Fe mysteries may have been solved. Our historian presents evidence that she believes is proof that the staircase was built by a wandering Frenchman who actually had many more tools to work with than a mallet and handsaw.

I don't know about you, but in this case I'm going to ignore my horse sense and throw away everything Mrs. Betty Graham taught me in elementary school science about logic, deduction, and evidence. I think I'd rather ignore the "new" evidence and continue to believe and perpetuate the legend of the mysterious carpenter. Yes, when it comes to Santa Fe's Miraculous Staircase, I'm going to take the dirt road.

But that magnificent staircase is obviously not our only "solved" mystery.

Of course, there is the mystery of the crashed flying saucer at a remote ranch near Corona that is now known as the "Roswell Incident." Although the military's official position is that all this unnecessary hoopla is over a downed weather balloon, many are still taking the dirt road on this one too, fervently believing that an actual UFO crashed on that remote south-central New Mexico ranch just northeast of the Capitán Mountains in 1947. And it's still a mystery to me why Roswell gets all the credit for that incident even though the city is more than 100 miles away from the crash site.

One night as I was driving home from a softball game at the Municipal Recreation Complex's Tom Aragon Fields, I rolled upon another mystery waiting to be solved. As I turned off onto the Veterans Highway, or NM 599, or the Santa Fe Bypass to most of us, and headed north, I noticed a white line right smack in the middle of the right-hand lane. As I continued to drive, I noticed this white line meandered throughout the lane and I was careful not to get mesmerized by its path, lest the driver behind me assume that I had partaken of too many Hamm's beers with the fellas that night after the game. Keeping an eye on the line, I assumed that its origin was perhaps from a leaking paint can in the back of some unsuspecting construction worker's pickup.

I assumed that the line would get more and more faint. But it never did, and instead of continuing to follow it, I turned off at my usual Camino de los Montoyas cutoff. A few weeks later I had business in Nambé and, sure enough, on the new highway to Pojoaque, there was that line again, drawing me into its spell. The line, never once really losing its luster, continued on its wandering path within the lane, then turned east onto NM 502 to Nambé, where I lost track of it after turning off near the church.

I pretty much forgot about this highway peculiarity until one day I was driving back from Albuquerque with a friend. Sure enough, in the right side of the northbound lanes near Bernalillo I happened to look down and there it was—that mysterious white line, just as pronounced as it was on the bypass as well as on the way to Pojoaque.

Yep, and just ahead of us there was a Subaru Outback with Colorado plates, its driver obviously hypnotized by the line's allure, following its meandering path. If I hadn't already known about this mysterious phenomenon, I would have assumed my Colorado friend had partaken of too many Fat Tires. Who knows, maybe this line leads to a large vat of Kool-Aid ready to be consumed by those foolish enough to be taken in by its spell?

Was this line the result of an elaborate hoax by some pranksters ready to be entertained until the state's next blacktop job? Or was it the oversight of some painter, who got out of his truck somewhere up north ready to paint some house white only to discover that his drum of paint had mysteriously disappeared on the way, much to the chagrin of his boss back in Albuquerque?

Maybe we'll never know, because to solve this puzzle, someone's going to have to follow the line's path while facing oncoming traffic and we all know where that's going to lead. No, this highway dilemma has all the classic makings of an intriguing New Mexico dirt-road mystery and that's exactly where I prefer to leave it. Besides, after several years of providing fascination, the line is long gone under the many repavings of the highway. But just like the giant Demon that lurks behind the many repaintings of the inside walls of Santa Fe High's Toby Roybal Memorial Gym, I know it's still there. And I am not alone!

Perhaps that's why the intrigue and mystery of Santa Fe is not all that pronounced any more. There just aren't as many dirt roads as there used to be.

Lookin' at the Letters

It's hard not to notice that there's an awful lot of movie-type trailers parked around town. Every time I happen to randomly pass one, my neck automatically turns to rubber in dramatic hopes of spotting a random movie star or perhaps a director or producer who might spot me for a bit part in the production. Never mind that my truck windows are tinted and the street-side cops quickly shoo-shoo me and the other gawking motorists away from the area

Oh well, it never hurts to dream of being in the movies, and if the camera adds ten pounds to your figure, that means I must lose fifty so that the cameraman can use a regular lens instead of a wide-angle. I realized a long time ago that Hollywood ain't exactly beating down the doors looking for a short, pudgy, balding guy who makes up for all that by being obnoxious. The late Don Rickles already had that niche tied up before political correctness made a comedic market correction.

When Jessica Simpson was in town shooting *Employee of the Month*, they had half the South Capitol district blocked off for filming. I'd cruise by slowly to maybe spot the fledgling actress. When I told my young sons what all the commotion was about, they also rubbernecked it, hoping to catch a view of Bart and Homer Simpson. I didn't have the heart to correct them.

Moviemakers have been coming to Santa Fe for as long as I can remember. The first movies I can vividly recall being filmed here were *The Cheyenne Social Club, Red Sky at Morning, Flap, Billy Jack*, and *The Cowboys*. The makers of each one of these popular '60s and '70s flicks always used plenty of locals as extras, and the shooting locations throughout town and in the vicinity were bountiful as well as recognizable.

Even today many people I know have been employed by movie productions as extras, skilled construction workers, or specialists in landscaping, makeup, and food preparation. At one time in my youth, I toyed with starting a valet parking service for the movies. I was going to call it "Valet, a la A" (pronounced locally as vah-leh, ah lah eh). But back in the 1980s, the movie productions came to town only once in a while and since at the time I already had bills in my name arriving regularly on my doorstep, I gave up on the idea of breaking into the big screen business and concentrated on my day job instead. That didn't stop others, however, and they continued to dabble in whatever infrequent jobs they could find in film production.

It is always a treat to make it into a packed downtown Lensic Theater where a motion picture shot locally makes its debut in the City Different. Believe me, if you're there to enjoy the picture with the complete silence and cooperation of those around you—fuggedaboutit! Catch another show time to watch the movie in peace.

You can always tell who the extras are in the crowd because they'll enthusiastically pull on their companion and whisper something loud like "Get ready, you'll see me right over . . . oh, man, they cut that scene out!" And sure enough, the rest of the night, this disappointed gentleman just doesn't seem as enthusiastic as he was when he first walked in.

I can still hear the collective sigh of many in the audience during the first screening of *The Milagro Beanfield War* at the Lensic one sunny Saturday morning in the mid-1980s when they showed the mountain village of Truchas for the first time in the movie.

"There's my Truchas!" a little old lady in front of me exclaimed proudly, clutching her companion's hand in the process. After that premier, you could pick out many of the Truchas locals in the theater because their faces had suddenly become familiar while the movie played on the big screen. And during this showing, just like at the Lensic debuts of *Red Sky at Morning, Flap, Billy Jack,* and *The Cowboys,* you regularly see people unabashedly pointing (and not just at the screen) and hear loud exclamations like "There I am!" or "Look, there's Johnny!" or "There's my car!"

But those who were working in front of the camera (and their relatives) are usually not the only ones in the audience. Just as many moviegoers hurry to get out of the theater in the same rush they were to get in, those locals (and visiting out-of-town crew members) who worked in the trenches behind the scenes are usually the ones who remain in their seats.

They patiently wait there after the movie not to get their money's worth but rather to "look at the letters," as my oldest son used to say when he began watching movies himself at that amusing age when he had just learned to talk but still couldn't read. These crew members usually applaud enthusiastically when their own name appears or that of someone they know. That is, of course, if the credits are orderly and legible and don't move too fast for someone who never took a speed-reading course.

And what am I still doing there in the theater, you might ask? Well, besides satisfying my own curiosity about which local resources and talent were used in the production, sometimes, if I'm lucky, somebody might have dropped a ten or a twenty on the floor in their zeal to get out, no doubt to a post-premier party at some swanky downtown nightclub. Either that or maybe some stray talent scout or producer lagging behind his party might still be in the theater on the lookout for the next George Constanza. Just kidding, bro!

But I did eagerly look at the letters when they premiered the movie *Wild Hogs,* which they filmed here. I looked for my friend Vince Pacheco's name next to a fancy title called "Food Stylist" or something like that. Vince regularly dished out grub to both cast and crew while they filmed scenes for the movie in Madrid. (I pronounce it "mah-threed" just so that locals over there can feel good about correcting my proper Spanish pronunciation and proclaim it's called MAD-rid.)

Vince revealed to me that there's one scene in the movie in which actor Tim Allen is situated in front of a sandwich with a bite taken out of it. However, through the magic of movies, that bite mark didn't come from ol' "Tool Time" Tim's chompers, but rather from Vince's. Yes, my food-stylist friend said he had to prepare and bite many sandwiches in the same manner while they filmed multiple takes to complete the scene. Boy, I sure hope Vince remembered to use wheat, romaine, and salami every time instead of rye, ham, and iceberg. Otherwise, we'll have to spot another local movie-blooper.

Yeah, just like the famous fight scene in *Billy Jack* where he says he's gonna take his right foot and kick the local patrón in the face and there's nothing he can do about it. Nothing wrong with the exciting fight scene where Billy eventually gets stomped by the patrón's posse of rednecks, except it was filmed in three different locations: the Federal Courthouse grounds in Santa Fe, the Las Vegas Plaza, and a park in either Portales or Clovis (I'm still trying to figure that one out).

There's another mix-up in *The Milagro Beanfield War* where the old man Amarante Córdova jumps on an earth-moving tractor in the Truchas beanfield, then drives it over a cliff around fifty miles away in the Jémez Mountains, all in a matter of seconds. And by the way, the piece of heavy equipment going over the mesa was not the one the old man was first driving through the beanfield.

So if you find yourself in the theater watching *Wild Hogs* and suddenly the guy in front of you excitedly points and yells, "Look, that's my bite mark in that sandwich," then you know that's my friend Vince.

And later, while you're looking at the letters and someone yells at someone else in the semidarkened theater, "Hey, that's my twenty!" then you know they're talking to me.

"I" before "E" except after "Oh Sí"

Throughout the years, there have been plenty of Santa Fe–area examples of life imitating art, or art imitating life, or life imitating art imitating life, or art imitating life imitating art imitating life, or whatever combination of that ol' saying you can copy-and-paste together to best suit your needs.

One high-profile episode, which was definitely hardscrabble life imitating art imitating life (I think), occurred in Madrid when an enterprising fella decided to capitalize on the publicity generated by the nationally released movie *Wild Hogs*. He wanted to ride the coattails of the movie to promote his own weekend musical extravaganza in the former mining-turned-ghost-turned-curio-turned-movie-set-turned-curio town.

Some folks didn't take too kindly to the entrepreneur's plans, especially since the town had just barely recovered from the real-life disruption caused by all the movie crews (or were those bikers?), their big trucks and equipment and all the noisemaking bells and whistles of a major filmmaking project. And do I need to mention all the trampled flower gardens and startled dogs and cats?

But the real Harley backfire heard round the county exploded when the promoter decided to spice up a planned cooking contest by spelling our sacred *chile* with an *i* instead of an *e*—you know, like in Texas chili. That's the way it's spelled in the rest of the nation too, where many still think these parts are a foreign country.

Heck, there's already an *i* in *chile*. Why do they need another? I still haven't gotten used to them calling more than one pepper "chiles" instead of just "chile," as in "I have to go, guys. I gotta go help my wife peel chile." Somehow it just doesn't sound right, peeling "chiles." And forget about all the times when the TV weatherman exclaims that it's "pretty chilly" and all your taste buds reply to the television, "Thank you!"

Personally, I was afraid that if they did spell *chile* the other way, they might have convinced our upstanding lawmakers to temporarily change the official state question as well. That's right, "Red or Green?" would have changed that weekend to "Mustard or Mayo?" Much more palatable to the rest of our hamburger-eating nation. And the official answer, you ask? Why, "Fourth of July," of course, a colorful splattering of both condiments, with maybe some Taco Bell hot sauce thrown in.

The last time a much heralded movie production stirred up a New Mexico dust devil like this was back in the mid-1980s when Robert Redford was in the state looking for a sleepy village where he could shoot *The Milagro Beanfield War*. His first choice was the plaza in historic Chimayó and, of course, the Chimayosos responded with a resounding and unified "¡*Chale!*" That's right, a Chimayó chale (local slang for "no") that ranks right up there with a Chimayó chile!

Local leaders felt all the rigmarole of Hollywood would have disrupted the community too much and maybe somebody with some pull would have started spelling Chimayó with an *a*. You know, like the way a lot of tourists pronounce it, "Chimaya."

Then, of course, another enterprising fella would have wanted to hold a mariachi concert in a fallow alfalfa field and call it "Chimayoberry, T.L.C." so that it also would sound familiar to the rest of our Andy Griffith–loving countrymen. Of course, the official question down at the nearby chile-dog stand would have been "Mustard or Chimayó?" And the official answer:"Cinco de Mayo."

Redford was disappointed, but he told the local papers that the community's refusal was a classic example of life imitating art imitating life. Or was that art imitating life imitating art? I still can't get that one straight, even after more than thirty years.

There's no doubt that coming to New Mexico and changing letters around isn't as easy as it used to be. Just ask the history buffs about Albuquerque, which used to have another *r*, as in *Alburquerque*. When I relate this story to interested friends visiting from Back East, I tell them that after the railroad rolled into the Duke City, "white man come and take *r* away!"

Then I tell them there's another centuries-old mystery about what happened to the *c* in Taos, which used to be known as Tacos before the strange disappearance. I once told this to a friend of mine from Taos. His reaction? "Oh, sí!"

Oh well. Maybe I should just stick to my own backyard, where now it's not uncommon to see the *a* dropped from Santa Fe, which becomes "Sante Fe" on too many occasions than we all care to admit. We're currently facing the dilemma of the sante-fication of the City Different, not to be confused with the prior Californication and croissantification of Santa Fe.

But there are even mysterious additions of letters in our history. For instance, when we were kids, we were always taught to spell Gen. Stephen Dubya's last name with another *e*—as in Kearney. Heck, they even had it spelled like that right there on the front of an elementary school for decades and on some of the street signs. But the poor American conqueror never spelled his name that way; he always wrote it as Kearny. And not only that, we've also been mispronouncing his name, because his relatives were in town a couple of years ago and they told everyone it is correctly pronounced "CAR-nee" not "KER-nee."

I didn't have the heart to tell them that they were standing under a Siberian elm, not a Chinese one, when they pointed out our mistakes. Because, as I tell my kids, it's not that they didn't teach me, it's just that they taught me wrong.

I'm sure somewhere out in the beautiful expanse of this state there is a buried treasure chest filled with all the letters lost and added from our beloved place names, nouns, and other descriptive phrases. I hope to find that chest one day, and who knows, maybe I'll find a few of my lost socks too! I'm sure the chest will still be there, even if someone finds it before me because the chest they will want is the one Forrest Fenn hid somewhere out there with valuable hardscrabble, not one with a bunch of forgotten letters!

And, by the way, I feel sorry for the next fella who rolls into town and tries to take one of our letters away. He's asking for a poke in the *i*.

Names That Stick to Your Craw

Back in the old college days when money was about as scarce as a regular home-cooked meal, I used to boil a lot of cheap spaghetti noodles. And that's usually when whoever was in the bare-cupboarded kitchen at the moment suddenly became an expert on the art of boiling pasta in hopes of getting a free meal. Perhaps the one thing that stuck with me the most was when one hungry onlooker, back by a pile of cracked peanut shells all over the floor, offered unsolicited advice about when you could tell when the boiling spaghetti noodles were done.

"All you do is get one out and throw it against the wall and if it sticks, the spaghetti's done," this freeloading housemate offered, no doubt anticipating the much awaited moment of truth when the Ragu sauce from the past weekend's visit to dear ol' Mom's house would complete the meal. "Here, let me show you!"

My new best friend for the moment grabbed a fork from the counter, fished out a single noodle, and then with his long finger chucked it toward the wall, where it stuck for a split-second before slithering down an inch or two and plopping to the floor. For the next several minutes, noodle after noodle came out of that boiling pot of water to the same result, and laughter.

Finally, one limp noodle flew up off his finger and instead of hitting the wall, it stuck to the high ceiling of the kitchen. In addition to telling us the spaghetti noodles were done, that one noodle remained there not only during the time it took us to scarf down that rare warm meal, but also for the rest of the semester and no doubt long after we housemates went our own merry ways. Heck, as far as I know, that curled spaghetti strand might still be up there on the high ceiling of that 12th Street kitchen in Las Vegas, New Mexico, nearly a half-century later.

The last time I drove by there a couple of years ago, the old Territorial-style multilevel brick house still looked pretty much the same as when we wintered there, freezing our *como se llamas* off every night and morning because we didn't have the dough to have the gas turned on.

For some reason I couldn't help visualizing that spaghetti moment when I first heard about the City of Santa Fe's dilemma about naming the Southside library. It seems that whatever noodle our city cooks threw at that building, it just wouldn't stick to the wall—in someone's craw, maybe, but not on the wall. And just like that overcooked noodle that's probably still on the ceiling of that former animal house in Las Vegas, there was still a name stuck to the wall at the downtown library, where some suggested we hurl a new noodle.

Now before most of you start thinking that I'm a few noodles short of a spaghetti plate, let me bring up this spicy meatball. There are many more buildings in town that have been named and renamed and it's getting to be quite a sticky situation when we want to throw a half-cooked noodle at anything new or old. Take the old Villagrá Building on Galisteo Street and Cerrillos Road. The name of that old state building was pretty funny around the time the drug Viagra exploded on the mainstream market. The working stiffs in there probably took the brunt of many jokes, until they kicked all of those state Game and Fish folks out and then added an enormous addition, only to rename the whole place the Paul Bardacke Complex.

Nowadays, the only ones who should be allowed to crack jokes about wet noodles sticking to the walls over there are those who work in what is now known as the Villagrá Wing, even though it's still called a building outside. This old section, which is the shell of the original structure erected in 1934, wasn't named after some stiff-neck living at the time, as we tend to do today. Rather, it was named for Gaspar Pérez de Villagrá, one of the colonists who traveled with Juan de Oñate and who wrote the epic poem *La Historia de Nuevo México*, one of the earliest written accounts of New Mexico.

Noodles flew all over town when our council decided to throw them at the front of the new convention center. For nearly a half-century, that corner of town had the longtime Santa Fe family name Sweeney associated with it. I've known many members of the fine Sweeney family while growing up here, and I admit that I went off half-cooked when that old noodle of a name came down for good at the same time the walls of that old gym came down.

I sure wanted to win the lottery then so that I could offer the city a million bucks so that people could book their events at the ¡Órale! Santa Fe Convention Center complete with the Sweeney Community Meeting and Gaming Hall.

But just as our former mayor said during the whirlwind of the Southside library-naming debacle, "fame is fleeting." So it was for Della's Place behind Wood Gormley Elementary School. The old wooden snack shack was unceremoniously bulldozed and now a fancy new guesthouse sits there, its new walls devoid of any noodles, graffiti, or mustard, for that matter.

No, we Harrington Junior High alumni never dared to stir up a gremlin's lair and demand they name the fresh structure "Della's Casita." I wonder if the present owner would ever take a million bucks to do just that and—¿quién sabe?—maybe even name the main house Guy P. Harrington as part of a no-sticky-noodles-attached donation.

Oh well, I think we could go on and on about Santa Fe place names and renames that never really stick because some of those old noodles just won't fall off the wall. Like Villa Linda Mall, or the Sheraton, or the Crown Building, or maybe the old hospital, or Mager's Field, or Canyon Road Park. All these places are called something else now, but we locals can't help calling them by their old names.

I guess that's the dilemma of the name game in a historic city like Santa Fe, where really old history gets covered up by mere old history, which gets covered up by recent history, which is now being covered up by soon-to-be history and pay-per-view history. It's just a fact of life that things that were and are important to us in our lifetime won't be as meaningful to our children and grandchildren and all the people getting off the bus in the future when the name-game baton is passed to the following generations.

I just know that when my kids start deciding to name things, I'm going to make sure they clean up all that damn spaghetti off the walls. Oh yeah, and the ceiling too.

Don't Blink or You'll Miss It

One time a friend of mine emailed me and pointed out that we're inevitably reaching that ripe old age when we're remembering more places in Santa Fe that are gone than are still here.

Of course I denied it at first. Then I thought maybe there was a point in there somewhere, if only I could remember it. But that might be the trait of considering yourself a bona fide *santafesino* or *santafesina*—the less widely used but local gender-correct words that predate the trendy moniker Santa Fean by a long shot.

You see, if you've been here long enough, it's pretty common to point out to newcomers, usually with pride, locations that no longer exist. Absence makes the heart grow fonder, as the old saying goes. Everywhere else in the good ol' USA where people get to that golden age, they usually retire to the front porch and watch the grass grow, that is, when they're not giving the finger to the passersby.

But here, we relish pointing out to people that they should have been here yesterday because it was so much better. You don't know the joy we locals derive from the astonished looks in people's eyes when we tell them that a gallery that used to be a home on Canyon Road could have been purchased for, let's say for laughs, $5,000 in the 1950s.

Never mind that the now nearly million-dollar-plus, expanded structure was originally a tool shed that was built from whatever scraps were left over from the construction of the main house, which doesn't exist now because it burned down when little Johnny first discovered stick matches. People today usually only find this out after they've invested a small fortune in the former shanty, where half an adobe wall came crumbling down below a leaky window while they simply wanted to replace an antiquated electrical outlet.

Then they become familiar with the city (and their neighbors) when they try to replace the original window, which was also a recycled construction scrap. But they are told they can't unless they replace it with a new one that authentically mimics the old one, which was really destined for the landfill had it not been for the need of a tool shed.

But that's part of the fun of becoming a local—all the stories, and the more embellished the better because who's going to question an old fogey out on the front porch with a finger at the ready? And the numbers of santafesinos are increasing and growing old nearly as fast as the disappearing locations of our youth. For instance, if you happened to get off the bus when the bus depot was still actually downtown, you just could be calling yourself a local by now. And you're probably pointing out that the old bus depot doesn't exist there any more on Water Street to all the others just off the bus who are enjoying expensive meals at the Coyote Café.

Ironically, the Coyote just happens to be situated above the old bus depot where the old twin-coney meal would fill you up for under a buck, before or after your long bus ride, a far cry from the prices charged over there now. But nowadays it's really hard to keep up with all the downtown shops that come and go, just like all the buses on St. Michael's Drive, where the bus terminal was relocated and now is also gone. Yes, my friends, today no one can technically be just off the bus in Santa Fe because the bus depot is now located out of town near Eldorado.

For a while there we didn't really notice the absence of the twin coneys at the original bus depot because we had the local Realburger hut just around the corner. But that, too, fell victim to the lucrative value of downtown real estate, which certainly doesn't overlook shanties. Luckily, original Realburgers as well as a whole gamut of other delicious dishes were available at the new restaurant on Old Pecos Trail in—you guessed it—what used to be the old Town House. And guess what, Realburger is gone from there now too! It's now on Maes Road. To be continued. . .

Okay, I know some places are still around and they've only just changed names, but many of us old geezers have a hard time coping with the new. Just like my mother-in-law usually says Burger Chef every time she's referring to Burger King, even though the artery-clogging, brain-jamming eateries weren't anywhere near each other.

Or like the time I was happily driving down the road and my youngest son, out of nowhere, asks, "Dad, do you like Cliff's?"

"Well, I really like to buy beer at Skaggs's or Payless or somewhere else where it's cheaper," I answer him.

"No, Cliff's, where the Roadrunner rollercoaster is," he clarifies to me.

"Oh, you mean Uncle Cliff's in Albuquerque. I thought you meant Cliff's Liquors." No wonder I thought it was odd at the time that this little second-grader knew anything about a liquor store. But one thing for sure is that he'll never know that amusement park as Uncle Cliff's unless he's talking to someone over 50. And Skaggs and Payless, I think those ones went right over his little head.

That sort of thing is becoming all too routine now when I drive around town with my kids. The other day I pointed out to them, "Hey, see those houses over there? We used to play baseball there, just like in that movie *The Sandlot*. Of course it was hard for them to visualize a ball field because of all the stacked and clustered condominiums, maybe twelve or so, on what used to be the four regular-sized lots that were standard for the old neighborhood.

But as some say, change is good, and it was especially good for whoever owned the four lots and it got better and better for everyone who flipped for the location thereafter. Luckily, we outgrew our sandlot days before the construction crews arrived. The only thing is that now most people have to drive the kids across town so that they can get a good game in before suppertime.

And if they're running late, they'll stop in at Burger Chef, uh, I mean King. But those joints will never beat the Realburger, which, thank gosh, hasn't gone the way of the twin coneys.

There aren't any more coneys in town, but there sure are a lot of cronies and they're usually not the kind you can easily stomach.

Stand and Be Counted

The old census numbers of 2005 tallied 66,453 people who called the city of Santa Fe home, while 137,758 people reported that they had their cribs set up in Santa Fe County.

Those aren't exactly staggering numbers when compared with New York, Hong Kong, or Río de Janeiro, but if you were a wee lad back when Santa Fe was still sleepy, those numbers are probably pretty intimidating. Yes, there are a handful of people still around who remember riding on a dirt road from Santa Fe to Pojoaque on a horse-pulled wagon and encountering as many other people as they could count on their hands and toes along the way—and perhaps two or three for the left big toe that was sticking out of the sole of their worn work boot.

And these same people will tell you that they remember the daylong ride to Albuquerque a few years later when their family was able to save enough money to buy a car. Of course, the notorious dirt road up and down La Bajada presented another set of problems, like getting stuck in the mud or having to climb its zigzagging grade backwards because the reverse gear was the only one with enough power to make it to the top.

I've heard many old-timers exclaim that those were the days when all roads leading in and out of Santa Fe were two-lane roads—one lane for the wheels on the right side and another lane for those on the left. These same people will attest that as the population of our fair city continues to rise, the number of jackrabbits and cottontails steadily declines. As the populace gains in numbers, the parking-violation fines follow suit with increases, but the number of available parking spaces seems to wane.

There has to be some kind of physics equation floating around in some file cabinet stuffed to the gills in Los Alamos that offers an analysis of population growth and its effects on the surroundings—northern New Mexico style. I'm sure one of those *listo* (smart) scientists commuting to the Hill from Ojo Caliente has thought about it once or twice while waiting on the road for the highway construction crews to get their giant earth movers the heck out of the way as they make the path wider for more people.

Ironically, in terms of that elusive norteño equation, it seems like the prairie dog population has increased along with our citizenry—quite the opposite of the other furry critters. I guess back in the day there weren't as many people to call the police when they saw someone go out to the ball field with their .22 rifle to take care of the cause of all those dangerous baseball-eating holes that kept appearing overnight in the outfield.

I know I'm not the only one who wonders if these latest population numbers are really accurate and if census takers were really able to count everyone. Take, for instance, the influx of Mexican immigrants who really don't want the US government to know that they're here or, perhaps, those stealthy recluses who live in the mountains, then move their camouflaged camp every time they sense other people in the area for any period of time.

I'll hand it to these census takers: it takes a lot of guts to go knock on a door after making it past a pack of growling Rottweilers while ignoring the Trespassers Will Be Shot! sign on the front gate. I remember one of those brave 1990 census takers who was counting the hearts still beating in the County Road 70 region west of Santa Fe, an area that before the days of the bypass (NM 599) was still considered way out in the boonies.

The counter, clipboard in hand, entered the barbed-wired, gated rural property ready to ask a laundry list of questions. Then he noticed in front of the ramshackle house the skeleton of a dog, which had a leash around its neck chained to a pole. After several unsuccessful attempts to get someone to answer the door, the suspicious census taker, who certainly had the willies by this time, called the county sheriff.

Deputies later found the decomposed body of the reclusive owner inside, where he had remained on the couch for years after committing suicide with a well-placed shotgun. Just like any person campaigning door-to-door for a politician during election time, a census employee is sure to tell you that you never know what you're going to encounter behind the next door.

I wonder if those 137,758 people who were counted in Santa Fe County include the ricos who periodically reside in the giant trophy homes in and around town that remain empty for most of the year. And these population numbers certainly swell up for our famous events throughout the year, for example, Indian Market every August. During my newspaper reporting days back in the mid-1980s, I remember one city official being grilled by a public safety committee member about how much the number of people in Santa Fe increased during such a world-renowned event.

The city official, puzzled at first, said it was pretty much impossible to give an exact number for the extra arms and legs and those of their dogs. However, he did point out that while he couldn't provide a people number, he could provide an accurate number for the increase in the hundreds of thousands of gallons of effluent treated at the city sewage treatment plant for the duration of such an event. They're especially busy over there at the facility at the end of Airport Road during that popular weekend.

There's no doubt that anytime you try to get an accurate number on every living, breathing person, an exact figure is going to be elusive, especially when you're trying to count part-time residents, tourists, and parents who owe child support. And forget about the number of babies who were just born during the time it took to read this cheesy column.

And by the way, they did come up with a seemingly accurate number for our statewide population at the time—1,887,200 New Mexicans. Now if I could only figure out how to get 1,877,199 of them to each give me a dollar.

Not Now, Kato!

I got a call from a friend while I was driving through a lightning storm and he told me in a serious voice over the cell phone, with wind and thunder clapping in the background and KBAC blasting on the radio, "I'm sorry about your *tío*. I heard he's not doing so well."

"What?!" I quickly replied, struggling to hear him through the particularly nasty weather while trying to hide my cell phone from the police squad car just up ahead.

"I said I'm sorry about your tío. I heard he's not doing so well," he repeated.

At least that's what I thought he said.

"What do you mean? Which one?" I was getting concerned.

"Your T. O. Terrell. Terrell Owens," he replied and not doing a very good job of holding back his laughter. "It seems like he's playing baby as usual on the sidelines."

"Man, you shouldn't do that. I thought you said my tío (uncle), not T. O.," I scolded back at him. "And besides, the Dallas Cowboys aren't even my team."

"I did say T. O.," he blabbed back at me. "I don't even know your tío. But you sure seem like a Cowboy junkie to me."

That's what you've got to expect in Santa Fe—the local banter among friends. Only in these parts we call it *carría* (cah-REE-ah), or good-natured teasing. I don't know about you, but it seems that not a day goes by without someone firing some type of carría salvo at me. And I'm not talking about ol' Sam, the former principal at E. J. Martínez Elementary School, who made me very acquainted with the disciplinary board of education back in the days when corporal punishment was not only legal but encouraged.

Carría can come at you when you least expect it, even in church. It can happen suddenly in the movies, in the checkout line at Smith's, in the bleachers at a Demon basketball game, while you're trying to bat during a softball game. And sometimes the good-natured insults come flying through the air no matter who you're with. Then before you know it, the people you're with join in on the carría at your expense.

I recently made friends with this guy down at the gym who hails from one of the northern pueblos. One day he was wearing a maroon T-shirt that announced in big letters SANTA FE INDIAN SCHOOL BRAVES PRIDE. I asked him if it bothered him that some teams were named after Native American themes like the Braves, the Indians, the Redskins, the Seminoles, etc., etc. He said that he's an avid follower of sports and that it never really occurred to him that such team monikers were offensive until it started appearing in the news, especially that item about a group of Native Americans from the Northeast who, in protest of such names, started calling their basketball team The Fighting Whities. He then asked me if I found any particular ethnic team names offensive.

"Of course I do," I told him matter-of-factly.

"Really, are you part Indian or something?" he asked.

"No," I replied, "but I am thinking of filing a class-action lawsuit against the Cleveland Browns."

We both laughed out loud, but I don't think the people within earshot of us found the wisecrack very amusing. My new friend caught on quickly to the idea of Santa Fe carría and he quickly revealed his northern pueblo version of banter as well. Now he tells people when I'm in the vicinity, "I'm not going to say anything because this guy's just going to twist it around."

Boy, I wish all my friends were like that. Most of them boast that they like to get off the first shot just so they don't start off any encounters at a disadvantage. You might call it our way of "exchanging unpleasantries" without saying hello or good morning or anything like that. Don't worry, though—usually when the insults come flying, it's because they like you and also they really get a twisted kick out of seeing your wife laugh at you too.

But don't get me wrong, if someone gets the advantage on you during a particular exchange, that gives you free rein to use the same advantageous ammunition during another encounter—with someone else! Good-natured theft it is, and it's been happening since mankind grunted the first insult at his fellow thumb-utilizing mammal.

Of course, there are times when somebody's just not in the mood for carría and it's best to just stay away. You better not mention that his T. O. isn't quite up to par. Otherwise, you might have a "carrían conflict" on your hands and you need to have an exit strategy somewhere among your offenses. And just maybe one day, it is indeed you who might not be in the mood for some wise guy cracking overused jokes about your tío even though you know he meant T. O. Remember: breathe, count to ten, think of a green meadow, and recall that famous line from the *Pink Panther* movies, "Not now, Kato!"

Do everything you can to prevent the sound waves from graduating from T. O. jokes to mama jokes because then you're one step closer to the *fregazos* (fisticuffs) piercing the air instead of the barbs. Yes, if the exchange turns from jibes to jabs, it usually means the end of carría as you know it with that particular person.

But don't confuse a "carrían conflict" with a "*corridan* conflict," which happened to me one day. I was at the gym and a doctor friend of mine (believe it or not) said to me, "Hey Arnold, are you going to the coh-ree-dah this weekend?"

"The what?" I asked, trying to act confused.

"The coh-ree-dah," he replied.

"What the hell is that?" I asked, again acting like I didn't know what he was talking about.

"The COH-REE-DAH!" he said, this time with more emphasis. "You know, the run. The Coh-ree-dah Day Santeh Fay."

"Oh, the *corrida* [coh-ree-thah]," I teased back at him. "Say it: coh-REE-thah."

"Coh-ree-dah," he grimaced.

"No, coh-REE-thah," I said again, only this time with the most macho, deep pachuco accent I could muster.

This could have gone on forever, but fortunately we both had an exit strategy for this "corridan conflict"—we both had to get back to work. There was no way in heck I was going to make this learned doctor say "thah" instead of "dah" or "sawn-tah" instead of "san-teh" without major voice training.

I didn't have time that day to really have some fun with him and get into the old "Rrrruffles have rrrridges" routine and really rrrruffle his feathers with some carría. And this was the same guy who could pronounce tongue-twisting medical terms, prescription drugs, and homeopathic remedies with ease, especially chondroitin glucosamine, which eventually took care of the stiffness in my voice box after that particular exchange.

I'm sure glad he's not going to be the physician in the room for my next physical examination because I'd surely be pronouncing T. O. in a different tone that day. Instead of taunting him about his T. O., I'd be calling him tío, especially when the bill came.

Siberian Elms: Plague of the Land

Where is the outrage? Have people been asleep? Why aren't the masses up in arms? Doesn't anybody care? I bet you thought I was talking about the wars in the Middle East, or the price of gasoline and construction materials, or perhaps the proposed school closings, or the last presidential election. No, I'm asking these questions because of something that's been going on for decades in these parts and a whole lot of people don't seem to care.

I'm talking about the unchecked growth of Siberian elms, or Chinese elms, as they used to call them back in the day before some retired dendrologist with too much time on his hands moved to town, called the local paper, and instructed a reporter to correct our misguided local arboreal classification, which had been embedded in our vocabulary for decades.

The other day as I was emptying my water buckets into my aspen trees and lilac bushes after one of those plentiful godsend downpours, one of my friendly neighbors commented to me with a smile, "We've got more water than we know what to do with, eh?"

I looked up at him from my new large-capacity green water barrel, which I proudly purchased from some ricos who were moving out of Las Campanas and had a yard sale, basically selling everything that wasn't bolted down. With sweat pouring down my brow and the front of my pants soaked with clean, freshly splashed rainwater, I replied, "Yeah, maybe I can use it to water all these baby trees in my yard that came from your tree."

"Heh, heh, heh," he snickered at me as he quickly walked back into his house. He already knows how I feel about Siberian elms. He and the other elm-loving neighbors seem oblivious to the devil seed that spreads, mostly uncontrolled, from these towering deciduous varmints every spring.

Of course, after I emptied all my fancy new barrels for about the umpteenth time—but I'm not complaining—I turned my attention to the pesky little sprouts that always seem to be everywhere. Oh, I thought, if only I had pulled out the power blower and sent the little white devil seeds back to where they came from, or at least in the vicinity, the moment I saw them adorning my yard with that unwelcome and familiar white speckling.

The ground was still wet from a recent cloudburst and I did my best to pull what I could, amazed once again at the resiliency of the sprouts. Some of them came right up, while others broke off at the root as it disappeared into the safety of the ground. I'll get it later with weed killer or my shovel, I thought, after every sound of a "snap." Then I unleashed a slew of cuss words that I am unable to repeat here.

It reminded me of the time one of my friends, a shade-tree mechanic at the time, was changing a throw-out bearing and clutch on my old 4×4 Ford F-250 pickup, also known as a civilian's tank. He was sprawled out under the truck and every once in a while he would shout out, "&*#@^%* Ford!!! [clank, clank] &*#@^% Ford!!!"

As I sat there patiently waiting for him to finish, I thought he was an ardent fan of Chevrolet products or perhaps Peugeot, judging from his French. Then all of a sudden he emerged from the ground and instructed me to follow him to the greasy void below.

"I want you to take this wrench and tighten up all those screws there, then tighten up all the bolts over here," he said as he pointed to the transmission and engine manifold.

I eagerly started the duty as he went away for some water, and before you know it, the wrench slipped and my hand went banging into one of the nearby hunks of metal, causing a scrape and some blood to appear on a finger. I continued on and the same thing happened several times over. Suddenly, as if by magic, every time the wrench slipped again, there I was too, "&*#@^% Ford!!! [clank, clank] &*#@^% Ford!!!"

Meanwhile, back at the ranch, I was able to pull up about half of my goal of elm sprouts for the evening before darkness saved the day for the rest of them. My children always laugh when I tell them I'm going to go outside and pull trees from the ground. That's right, it's backward at my house: I call the elm sprouts "trees" and the full-grown ones "weeds."

Either way, the unchecked Siberian elms have drastically changed the countryside in northern New Mexico and it seems like it's getting worse. Now in my older years I have stopped calling them weed patches and refer to them instead as Chicano rainforests! One of my favorite photographs is *Moonrise, Hernandez, New Mexico,* by Ansel Adams. I remember, when I was a boy, my father pointing out to me more or less the same location where the picture was taken back in the 1940s. Every time I pass the same spot today on my way to Chama, it's always a challenge to find the angle because of the overgrowth of Siberian elms. Also, it's darn near impossible now to spot the church and graveyard from the car going sixty mph.

I never stop anymore because I read what happened to one of the Imus brothers a few years back when he tried to take a photograph from the same angle and one of the neighbors in the area shoo-shooed him away, much to his displeasure. He told his brother Don Imus what happened and before you know it, they were broadcasting some pretty disparaging remarks about the people around here, sort of straying from their original beef.

Okay, I admit if anyone today manages to get off a shot of the church from Ansel's same angle, the contemporary photo probably would better be titled *Moonrise Over Shotgun Barrel, NM,* or *Moonrise Over Siberian Elm Trees, NM,* or maybe *Moonrise Over Tingley's Disease, NM.*

I've always heard rumors, or maybe they were urban legends (or arbor lore, if you will, like Jack and the Beanstalk), that the late politician Clyde Tingley was the one who introduced the first fast-growing elm trees to New Mexico back in the 1930s because they provided rare deciduous shade to our then called Sunshine State. I'm tempted to say that because of him things have been shady in New Mexico ever since, but my studies of political science indicate otherwise. Things were shady here long before Gov. Tingley planted his first invasive weed from the East.

In fact, ask anyone who owns one of those towering elm weeds why they never chop it down and they'll almost always tell you, "Because it gives such good shade." True. But to me it's like asking someone why they keep a mean, vicious pit bull chained in the hot sun to a pole in their front yard all day. They almost always say, "Because he's a good watchdog."

To paraphrase a local bumper sticker, if you're not outraged by Siberian elms, you're not paying attention. Another sticker phrase also applies: you should "think globally, act locally," at least in the locality of your front and back yards.

Oh, and incidentally, the other day I went home for lunch and saw an open Roto-Rooter truck parked in front of my friendly neighbor's Siberian elm tree by the street, the driver nearby motoring a sewer snake into the home's cleanout pipes.

"Heh, heh, heh," I snickered to myself as I walked into my house.

Part 4
Agua Fría

Hundreds, if not thousands, of motorists in a hurry to get from one side of town to the other and then quickly back again probably have no idea that Agua Fría Street once was the end of an arduous northern journey from Mexico City on a series of paths known as El Camino Real and the Chihuahua Trail.

Wild in the Streets of Santa Fe

A short time back, I found myself on more than one occasion cautiously looking around from side to side with a tingle of bona fide fear running up my spine.

No, it wasn't the time a couple of what looked like teenagers in the car in front of me took exception to my honking at them for not turning left onto a side street of St. Francis Drive after the way was clear for about ten seconds. Before you know it, after the bleep of my horn and their ensuing obligatory hand gesture, one of them got out of their car and retrieved a baseball bat from the trunk. I honestly don't believe he wanted me to pitch them some baseballs for practice swings in traffic before the big game.

Nor was it the time when a person among a carload of young men began yelling across the street at me and a couple of friends who were watching a youth athletic contest at a crowded Westside park. The young man, upset that a few of the fans decided to park their cars in front of his house because there was nowhere else to park, screamed at us that we should go tell those people to move their cars. Otherwise, he was going to slash their tires.

Since I didn't happen to have a loud speaker and microphone with me at the time to broadcast to the, uh, one- to two-hundred people cheering around the field, I could only yell back at the angry resident that I didn't really know who the cars belonged to. He didn't like my answer and he yelled some more not-so-nice things at me before his friends coerced him into the house. Thankfully, he never emerged again from that happy home to fillet some Michelin à la BMW, at least during the time we watched the game.

An occasional encounter with a group of testosterone-spewing men is to be expected not only in Santa Fe but also in any town that allows boys coming of age to drive automobiles. As the mighty matador philosopher once said, "it is best to get out of the way in order to live another day."

No, the fear that once became my uneasy companion was born of a much more honorable creature than any fledgling macho man. I feared the mountain lion that somehow decided that city slicker, can-fed housecats and neighbor-irritating chickens and roosters were easier pickings than his usual delectable meals of wild mice, jackrabbits, deer, and an occasional prairie dog too slow to make it back into his hole.

And my fear of the stealthy mountain lion wasn't only for myself, but more so for my own grade-school-age children, whom I had just managed to coerce away from the PlayStation during the sunshine of the day and consistently go outside to enjoy the great outdoors. Now that the mountain lion was on the loose, it was the backyard only for the brats, and we kicked the dog out there too so that he would spot and occupy the mountain lion in case of a midday encounter. Luckily, nothing ever transpired, but it was a good lesson for all of us that we still live in the natural world.

A friend of mine married a woman from Montana and after the first couple of visits to her family, he said he had to buy himself a .44 Magnum handgun. "Man," I told him, "she sure must come from a rough family."

"No," he laughed back at me, "I bought the gun as protection against moose and grizzlies. They're both known to attack people up there."

I'm not ready yet to go and buy an elephant gun because of a few mountain lion sightings. I'm afraid I'd be more inclined to use the firearm at one of those impromptu baseball games on St. Francis Drive than for a rare backyard cougar visit.

Another friend and his wife used to be caretakers for some ricos at a giant hillside house on the Eastside overlooking the city. For seven months out of the year the couple had it made because the owners lived at their other house in New York City. The caretakers essentially had the estate all to themselves. But when the owner came to their part-time autumn home, my friends sure had to earn their money. One autumn day when the ricos were home, my friend was startled midmorning when suddenly his boss started yelling at the top of his lungs. My friend emerged from the adjoining caretakers' quarters into the great room, which had a big picture window overlooking the grassy yard, the tennis court, and the panorama of Santa Fe.

"Hey, is that a mountain lion?!" the owner asked my friend. "There, on the tennis court, is that a mountain lion?!"

Now my friend, who has a better poker face and more restraint than I do, quickly realized that the so-called mountain lion was actually just the neighbor's overweight cat, a gray-striped, can-fed Morris that only slightly resembled the leaner, more noble bobcat. This overfed feline, he said, often waddled across the tennis court because it was too lazy to climb the adjoining hill back to its own yard. But his city-slicker boss didn't know that because he and his wife were rarely there.

"I don't know. It might just be a cat," my friend politely told him, probably more out of job security than anything else. Of course, his cynicism came out later when he snickered to us, "It was just a big fat cat that could barely move."

I think of that story every time I'm chomping down one of those juicy burgers at the Bobcat Bite, at least when it was still open over there on the Old Las Vegas Highway, where real mountain lions would be more inclined to hang out.

My fear was eased when sheriff's deputies downed the same young mountain lion in a neighborhood near the penitentiary. The wildcat fit the same general description of the one running loose in town—and my own *barrio*—that had everyone so concerned for a couple of weeks.

But our cougar worries pale in comparison with what the citizens of Las Vegas had to endure one year. Someone on the western fringes of that town claims he actually saw a chupacabra (goat sucker), a fabled beast in Latin America that viciously sucks the blood from animals, then disappears mysteriously.

No one's ever spotted the fierce bloodsucker in government-laden Santa Fe. There's probably too much competition here.

These Snacks Are Killing Me

In the years after I finished college, every once in a while I would awaken in the middle of the night from a recurring dream that got my heart pumping and my worry warts itching. It usually took a couple minutes of lying there in a cold sweat for me to realize that my frantic awakening had actually been caused by a bad dream that always seemed to be as real as the tax collector every April. No, there weren't any monsters or repo men involved, nor were there any ex-wives or football coaches.

Rather, I used to wake up in a panic that I was a second-semester senior in college and my academic adviser had informed me I couldn't graduate because I had failed to take just one course required for my major. So there I was, going back and forth in my head wondering and worrying if I had, indeed, taken that "Introduction to Law" requirement for the political science major.

My mood during those rude awakenings always reminds me of that old Dunkin' Donuts commercial where in the dark wee hours of the morning, a bath-robed baker is pacing back and forth in front of his bed muttering to himself, "Time to make the doughnuts, time to make the doughnuts."

After I left my job as a *Journal North* reporter back in the late 1980s, I actually took a job as a newspaper carrier for the *Journal* as a part-time gig. Yes, I used to tell everyone who knew me that I got a promotion— from reporter to paperboy. Carriers, as you may know, also have to awaken at 3 or 4 in the morning to be ready to get their newspaper bundles off the truck from Albuquerque. Then they must wrap the newspapers individually and throw them to each house and business on their routes before 7 a.m. Any carrier will tell you that dealing with an irate early-bird customer who doesn't get his paper by 7 a.m. is really a nightmare come to life.

So there I was at 3:30 in front of my own bed every morning, even Thanksgiving, Christmas, and New Year's, muttering to myself, "Time to throw the papers, time to throw the papers." In fact, just last night I suddenly awoke to find myself muttering, "Time to write a cheesy column, time to write a cheesy column."

It's been a while since I had that familiar college-credit nightmare, but nowadays I often wake up in a cold sweat from a panicky dream of a different sort. Now in my parenthood years, my early morning panic attacks have taken on a new twist. My frantic nightmares of late are more along the lines of "Were we the ones who were supposed to take drinks and snacks to Junior's soccer game yesterday?!!!" I don't know about you, but for me, the fear, embarrassment, and hurt suffered from not taking snacks to Junior's athletic contests are enough to cause severe late-night panic attacks.

Once, our snack turn sneaked up on us and, of course, we were unprepared ten minutes before game time. Let's see: three pint-sized Juicy Juices and a couple of Gatorades in the refrigerator and three little packages of peanut butter crackers in the cabinet left over from what they handed out at Junior's last game. "We're not going to make it!!!" I worried.

Since it was a snack emergency, I even entertained thoughts of parting with my own fancy case of Vienna sausages we had just bought at Sam's Club. My wife, however, put her foot down on that one. I guess she didn't want to see the disapproving looks on all the other soccer moms' faces when she handed each red-faced, hip-high player a plastic fork and his own little can of Vienna sausages after the game.

Luckily, an Allsup's was on the way to Junior's game and saved the day—until the next time. I wonder what the ancianos did in their day when snack day crept up on them and convenience stores and little cans of Vienna sausages had yet to be invented. Something tells me they had other things to worry about.

In my pint-sized playing days, snacks for sporting participants were quite different. Back then, you had to hit a home run or score a touchdown to earn a snack or a drink, and trophies were handed out based on performance rather than participation.

Yep, times have changed and it seems that every other day, we parents are getting hit up for snack donations, pizza party donations, jersey donations, trophy donations, league fees, equipment fees, candy sales, gift-wrapping sales, bake sales, book sales, team sales, and then, when we think it's all said and done, pictures, and they aren't cheap. It's enough to make you want to tell your kid to concentrate on one sport and one sport only, unless your loan comes through.

Man, they're killing me. I barely have enough left over to buy a case of Vienna sausages for my own snack emergencies anymore. The last time a parent organizer hit me up for uniform dough, I politely asked her if I could pay in deer meat or, perhaps, discount coupons. I had already used up the old food stamps and garden produce routine. (It's a good thing she didn't take me up on the deer meat offer, because I don't even hunt.)

My dad once told me that when he and his brothers were first getting ready to go to school at St. Mike's back in the 1940s, my rancher grandfather tried to get the Christian Brothers to accept freshly butchered meat and farm-grown produce as tuition payment. It would be a brothers-to-brothers bartering arrangement, or so he hoped. Of course, the Christian Brothers declined and demanded cash instead. I'm sure there were many times after that in the 1940s when my Grandpa woke up in the middle of night thinking, "Time to sell a cow, time to sell a cow," except in Spanish.

Well, I know that I'm going to sleep well tonight, especially since this column is done and I have two weeks until my late-night stress over the next one. Maybe I could even hand out little baggies of leftover Thanksgiving turkey for snacks at the next peewee athletic contest.

And You Can Quote Me on That

One time I was doing some research during the course of my day job and I happened to talk to this pleasant young lady who was speaking on behalf of the Taos Country Club.

As I asked her several questions about the specifics of the scenic golf course, she all of a sudden proclaimed with conviction over the telephone, "We have 365-degree views, 360 days a year."

Hmmm, I thought to myself. I knew she had just let go with an inadvertent slip of the tongue and she kept talking, unaware of what she had just said. After we ended our conversation, I looked at my notes and, sure enough, she did say that. For some reason, that brief verbal snafu stuck in my craw and I think I thought about it at least "seven hours a day, twenty-four days a week," or 7/24 as the old bungled saying goes.

As most of us who work in the world of journalism and media will attest, such incidents of obvious tongue-twisting occur from time to time and it sometimes comes down to the reporter's choice whether to print such comments verbatim or write down the quote as the speaker actually meant to say it. Some newspapers require their reporters to quote their sources word for word, regardless of intent, and then insert a "[*sic*]" where the verbiage gets murky. There's nothing like the feeling of a chill going up your spine when you know a reporter is going to [*sic*] you.

Now I knew what the young lady was trying to say and I didn't print what she actually said (until now) because I was compiling a concise description of the golf course for a pretty dry reference guide that left no room for silly judgment calls. But back in my hard-news days (that's media talk for former hard-nosed reporters before they turned soft and started writing cheesy columns and compiling boring informational guides), I probably wouldn't have let her slide. I guess back then I would have delighted in letting people think she meant that for five days a year there are absolutely no views at the Taos golf course. And that players would eventually end up with a five-degree neck ache after soaking up the beautiful panorama during their round of play.

Bungled quotes are part of the newspaper business, and for the entertainment of the readers, the more outrageous the better. Just ask onetime presidential candidate John Kerry about his slip of the tongue while talking on camera to a group of university students, saying that if you don't hit the books hard, "you end up in Iraq." He later apologized and called it a botched joke, but the media in this case had it all on video and there was no room for a compassionate writer's leeway.

If I had some extra dough to blow, I think I'd print up some bumper stickers in Kerry's honor and hand them out for Christmas: "Life's a Botch!" That's right, life's a botch and then you get [*sic*].

But we don't have to look throughout the country and across the globe to find interesting quotes when we have plenty right here in Santa Fe. Remember the olden days when former mayor Debbie Jaramillo was great for slinging a doozy or seven at the media, whether unintentional or not. I still recall when the reporters spotted her illegally parked Jaguar in a downtown loading zone for an extended period of time. When a reporter later asked her about it, she replied, "I was loading my stomach." But the juicy quotes that routinely came out of the mayor's office seemed to end with Debbie "he just got off the bus" Jaramillo and Sam "Santa Fe's a great place for a taco and a margarita" Pick.

I think the only raucous thing I recall coming from the mouth of the mild-mannered and gracious Larry Delgado was during a televised City Council meeting. After patiently listening to a barrage of criticism from a speaker during a public comment session, he somewhat heatedly chastised the critic by saying, "I've forgotten more about engineering than you'll ever know." Delgado's uncharacteristic choice of words never made it into the newspapers, but they did send a ripple of sound waves through the public-access channel into my face. I always wondered why the reporters there never asked him if he was having trouble with memory, a subject most politicians prefer not to remember (along with term limits).

Another person who was always reliable for a memorable quote or two was former municipal judge Tom Fiorina. One time after the actor George Kennedy was arrested on suspicion of driving tipsy on Cerrillos Road near Don Diego Avenue, Fiorina released the famous character actor on his own recognizance. Kennedy explained to the judge that he had never been arrested on such charges before and he committed an unusual U-turn because he was confused by the Santa Fe streets. The actor promised to take care of court matters at a later date.

After Fiorina explained the situation to me while I was working as a reporter covering the story, he mused out loud, "I hope to hell he ain't lying." The judge never took back his statement and those words made it into print. Now, I just "hope to hell he ain't reading this." By the way, the late Kennedy turned out to be on the level and he took care of his obligations just as he promised the judge, who was always good for quotes during his court sessions. There were the times I heard him say, "I'm going to dismiss these parking violations on the condition that you buy this young lady with you a steak dinner," or "I'm going to dismiss your ticket on the condition you bring in a turkey for the poor."

These were popular comments among the people in the "people's court," but they generally made lawyers, judges, and city bean counters cringe. These days, city parking tickets are still being dismissed, but they're being dismissed by someone with a law degree and not someone with a lot of voting cousins. The only difference is that there's no meat being exchanged.

Now come on—u [sic] people know what I mean, so don't quote me on that!

Enrique Sarcate

For decades, either in the newspapers or through books and published essays, many writers around these parts have written a whole lot about one special northern New Mexico character or another who made a lasting impression on them.

One writer even conjured up a popular newspaper column that later was published as a book about one of these fictional characters, whom he named Adobe Joe, while another wrote a book mostly about a real norteño who served as mayordomo of a small village ditch association.

Of course, one of the most famous characters of this ilk was named Joe Mondragon, that "pint-sized" SOB who caused all the trouble in *The Milagro Beanfield War*. Even in decades-old issues of *New Mexico Magazine*, there was a seasoned old hombre named Don Plácido who doled out statewide travel information tinged with a splash of local wit and wisdom in each installment.

I'm sure there were similar salty characters from publications down south who gave out the same type of advice and life lessons from a bow-legged cowboy's perspective. Cowboy wit is the stuff of legend in the West and it's always difficult to ignore a witty anecdote.

Back in college, when my motorcycle was my main mode of transportation, I came across one of these old witty characters when my steel horse broke down and left me stranded right smack on the outskirts of a small northern New Mexico village. There was nothing I could do at that point but hit the pavement and head for the nearest house to borrow the telephone. Walking along the road, I came upon an old adobe house with a rusty tin roof. As I walked up the driveway, an older man enjoying the late afternoon shade of his side porch surprised me.

"¿Qué quieres? [What do you want?]," he asked in a deep, resonating voice before I had a chance to offer greetings.

"My motorcycle broke down right over there by the curve," I replied in my most helpless, distressed voice. "I was wondering if I could use your phone to call for help."

"*Pues*, okay, it's right there in the living room," he said, pointing to the front door. "Just don't be calling China or anything. Or Española either. That's a long distance call."

"I won't. It'll be a local call," I reassured him. "Besides, I don't know anyone in China."

After I called a friend with a pickup to come and get me, I went back outside and joined the *viejito* outside on his porch, which overlooked a small garden and cornfield that glistened in the golden light of the receding sun.

"That's quite a cornfield you have there," I commented. "Is it a lot of work?"

"I've been planting this corn since I was a little boy," he replied. "The corn used to grow really big, but then they built that gosh darn Lo Hálamo and it didn't grow so big no more."

My new friend didn't pronounce Los Alamos the way we're used to hearing it being pronounced. After hearing him say it several times, it was not hard for me to start saying Lo Hálamo, especially with a pronunciation at the beginning of the second word (loh HAH-lah-mo) that sounds like you're clearing your throat.

"Really?" I answered. "Do you really think something that they're doing up there is causing your corn not to grow?"

"Pues, I can't prove it, but the corn was really big and long back in the old days," he said. "And after they built Lo Hálamo, we would always hear these big explosions coming from the mountains up there. It sounded like thunder, but there weren't any storm clouds in the sky.

"Then, all of the sudden we started to get these big cracks on the side of the house. And every year since, we've had to mix up some mud or cement and patch them up."

Coincidentally, I just happened to be working up at Los Alamos as a student intern at the time and when I wasn't carpooling up to the Hill from Santa Fe with some other people, I would take my motorcycle. After I met my new friend, I would always stop to say "Hola" to him if I saw him out on the porch from the road whenever I was by myself.

Oh yeah, and from then on, every morning when I saw my familiar carpooling companions in the morning, I would greet them by saying, "Bah-mo pah Lo Hálamo!" (Vamonos para Los Alamos, or "Let's go to Los Alamos," for you purists out there) while I clapped the back of my right hand against the palm of the left for emphasis. Sure enough, after a few rounds of this, you can bet the whole carpool began reiterating "Bah-mo pah Lo Hálamo!" every time we saw each other in the morning, and for some time after that, come to think of it.

The good folks up there never did offer me a permanent job after I graduated from college and my internship was over. That job went to the daughter of my former boss's friend. I often wonder if I'd still be working up there today, some thirty-five years later, if only I just hadn't started clapping my hands and saying "Lo Hálamo" so freely in LANL staff meetings. And as I mentioned before, I didn't know anyone in China, so my being a security risk wasn't a factor.

I'd certainly be driving a nicer car than I do now if I still worked there, but I certainly wouldn't have as much chisme (local gossip) and chiste (street humor) for these cheesy columns either. Oh well, I guess only the Lo Hálamo gods know for sure why back in the early 1980s they declared, "There shall be no Vigil working on the Hill."

Luckily, I was able to meet my new friend during my brief stint at commuting up to Lo Hálamo, and he didn't mind my calling him Enrique Sarcate (sahr-CAH-teh) every time I stopped thereafter to visit him, even though that wasn't his real name. I told him I liked *sarcate* because it was the closest thing to the word *sarcasm* I could think of during our first meeting.

Sarcate was only fitting because I could never tell if he was pulling my leg or not whenever he would tell a story or answer a question. Case in point: one time he told me about the first Anglo family that moved to his Spanish-speaking village when he was growing up.

"Man, when they first moved here, those little Anglo kids sure were smart," he said

"Really, why did you think that?" I asked him curiously.

"Because they already knew how to speak English."

Then there was another time when he pointed out that a hippie family had bought the village's old adobe church, renovated it, and begun using it as a home.

"Do you think God is still in there with them?" I asked.

"No way! They kicked God the hell outta there a long time ago!"

Later on, I asked him if I could have his cell number so that I could call him without making a long distance call. "Can I have your cell number so I can program it into my phone?" I asked.

"Cell number?" he asked back, pretending to look at me puzzled. "What makes you think I'm going to the *pinta* [prison]?"

Another time I asked him how his health was doing and if he ever went to the doctor. "No," he said. "Every time you go to the doctor, you come back sicker. Besides, it costs too much."

"But you could get some cheap insurance," I told him. "What do you think about HMOs?"

"*¿Qué?*" he asked back, cupping his hand to his ear

"HMOs," I said back to him in a louder voice. "What do you think about HMOs?"

"Pues, I don't have nothing against them, as long as they don't date my brother."

Well, he wasn't letting on that he understood what I meant about health care, so I tried a different approach on the subject he was referring to. I asked him what he thought about the ongoing movement of the LGBT.

Once again he cupped his ear and asked, "*¿Qué?*"

"L-G-B-T, what do you think about equality for the L-G-B-T?" I asked again, slowly and loudly, while getting closer to the side of his head.

"Ohhh, pues, at first I wasn't really comfortable about it," he answered me matter-of-factly. "But once I tried it, it didn't taste like yogurt at all!"

Every time, Señor Sarcate would answer in a serious voice, but that grin and mischievous gleam in his eye gave him away. Like the time I asked him where he stood on abortion and he replied, "Pues, behind the doctor, of course."

The last time I drove by his casita, he wasn't there on his usual perch on the porch and his cornfield was fallow. Nobody answered the door, but there seemed to be a lot of new stuff around his yard since the last time I visited.

Perhaps, I thought, he gave up on the corn and went to work up in Lo Hálamo.

Spring Runoff and Common Ground

In New Mexico having a great winter means getting a major snowstorm every week, just like the good old days when the word "drought" only applied to the chronic losing seasons of the Detroit Lions (and now the Oakland Raiders).

And come spring, sometimes early sometimes late, our familiar friend the sun routinely shows his bright face and quickly melts the few remaining north-facing snow banks. This change of season also means the chronic complainers write fewer letters to the editor about the hardworking city-street-clearing crews—though they are still upset about the leftover potholes, mounds of road salt, and actual founding date of our fair city.

With all the change-of-season dynamics, both natural and manmade, there's usually only one fantastic thing remaining: spring runoff. Now most of you probably first think of the runoff that causes our nearby riverbanks to swell to capacity with fresh snowmelt, draining en masse from our high mountains that received an above-average winter dump of the fluffy white stuff.

That's right, in such years, El Niño acts like El Niño instead of El No Snow.

But in my corner, spring runoff mostly means one thing—and it's not putting on the ol' lifejacket and jumping into a wobbly, air-filled raft with a bunch of other pasty fellas with farmers' tans and holding on for dear life down the fast-moving waters of the Río Grande. No, spring runoff for me means dusting off the old running shoes in the closet and taking good old "Fido" for a run up the nearest arroyo to start losing the extra baggage (or should I say flabbage?) I picked up over the cold season.

Spring runoff is quite necessary for me every warming season after many nights in front of the fire (or, more likely, the TV) downing sweets, spirits, and foods too rich for my aging arteries from Halloween, Thanksgiving, Christmas, New Year's, the Super Bowl, Valentine's Day, Easter, and all the rugrat and/or viejito birthdays and Girl Scout cookies in between.

There should be no excuses for not pounding the pockmarked pavement during the festive seasons of late fall and winter, but when it's cold and snowing outside, there's no better excuse than to contribute more to the coffers of the Budweiser, Hershey, and Posa families. For those of you who are confused, that means beer, chocolate, and tamales were far more appealing than freezing my *como se llama* off out in the inclement weather.

A few years ago I discovered this magnificent and isolated arroyo where I could run bare-chested and beer-bellied without fear of blinding drivers, scaring little old ladies, and grossing out beautiful women. In fact, this arroyo even afforded Fido the opportunity to run free himself, right alongside the jackrabbits and coyotes we often saw during my hurried noontime waddle.

We carried on this blissful spring ritual for many seasons, sometimes year-round, without ever really seeing anyone else except, maybe, the gentleman we startled under a bridge just after he lit up his *chootie*. In fact, we often saw footprints from other joggers and hikers and even some interesting cairns that seemed to regularly reshape themselves into interesting forms, but never any humans.

Then one day—I believe it might have been during one of my spring runoffs—we came upon this woman with a clipboard and topographical map in hand. I nodded greetings to her and she responded with a cursory lecture about how I needed to keep ol' Fido on a leash. Of course, being the good citizen that I am, I quickly leashed up my friendly mongrel and continued up the scenic arroyo as I always had in the past. On the way back, I encountered the woman again and she struck up a conversation with me. She asked me if I ran through there often and I replied, "Not often enough" as I rubbed my belly and put on my shirt to be polite. I told her this arroyo is one of the last places in town where freedom still seems to reign.

"Well, it's going to get better for you," she replied, pointing to her topographical map, which she was marking with notes of the physical surroundings. She said the area was one of the last major pieces of open acreage owned by the city on the Eastside, and the Santa Fe Botanical Garden was in negotiations to lease the arroyo located near Museum Hill to create pathways and colorful vegetation plots for many, many more visitors to enjoy.

"Hmmm," I thought to myself, "better for me?" Here Fido and I have this beautiful, seemingly isolated arroyo to run free through and soon there will be pathways, gardens, and more people. I wondered if it would also be better for the jackrabbits and coyotes.

I asked her if there was any opposition to the project from the nearby neighbors on Camino Lejo and Camino Piñones, whose backyards abut the arroyo. First she looked surprised that I would dare ask such a question and then she said she didn't think any of them would mind.

"Hmm," I thought to myself again. I wondered if the folks who had their fantastic, decades-old view of Sun Mountain blocked by the two-story state Cultural Affairs administration building on Museum Hill were going to mind, or all the other neighboring folks who opposed the same project from the start.

Oh well, living here in Santa Fe, I've already gotten used to so many of my favorite spring-runoff spots getting "better for me," basically forcing me to find another place to feel free for about an hour without having to pay the property taxes or deal with the lectures of letting Fido stretch his legs off the leash when no one is around.

In my three decades of battling the bulge during spring runoff, I've been shoo-shooed away from the arroyos at the end of Valley Drive, the mountains around Wilderness Gate, the hills where the houses at Pueblos del Sol now sit, the *cerritos* of Nava Ade, and many other formerly open areas now blocked by fences, walls, or houses. Even now, the fenced hills above the city near the old landfill are only dusty memories where the pounds used to melt away like magic during spring runoff.

There's an eerie pattern of familiarity to what many of the real estate pamphlets call "increasingly hard-to-find acreage" in Santa Fe. When somewhat isolated areas are discovered after other open areas become inaccessible, first the four-wheeler tracks appear over the old foot trails, then the remnants of bonfires and piles of discarded party containers appear, and, inevitably, the scattered mounds of trash from illegal dumping soon follow.

Then a few token ruts are dug to prevent the illegal off-roading, but resourceful 4-by-4ers always seem to find another way in, wearing down their struts and nobbies as well as the virgin landscape. After a few years of the increase of trash and off-road tracks, as well as the occasional discovery of a dead body, the scattered red-and-yellow survey markers appear, soon to be followed by a bright-yellow Public Notice sign.

Then you know it's only a matter of weeks before spring runoff must be performed somewhere else. We've been spoiled in Santa Fe, where one used to be able to enjoy spring runoff nearly anywhere in the city, from your own front door, without having to drive anywhere. Them days are gone, my friends.

With every new year my knees and hips make it harder to enjoy spring runoff, so the lack of free, open areas around the city is becoming less of a problem for me. As the pain increases, I just might have to contribute to the coffers of the Ross family for a larger set of trousers with an expandable waist, then enjoy spring runoff like most everybody else—with a picnic basket on the side of the Río Grande.

Either that or go on a diet and show some restraint during an El Niño year.

Kids Listen When Heads Roll

Sometimes it's hard not to take for granted that centuries of history literally ooze from the streets here in Santa Fe. I don't know how many times I've driven back and forth and up and down Agua Fría Street and it rarely dawns on me that this sometimes narrow thoroughfare once was the main dirt path leading into Santa Fe from "civilization."

By "civilization" I mean Mexico City, which for centuries was the epicenter of Spanish civilization in the New World. For some odd reason, I thought of this as I was driving west on the street one day with my twelve-year-old son. Thinking back, however, I must admit I purposely brought up the history of the street just to change the subject of his usual conversations about video games.

"You know what, Dad?" he asked me for the umpteenth time, "*Gears of War* could really happen 300 years from now."

"And you know what?" I quickly replied to him before he could get to the follow-up words I had heard from him so many times before, "This road once was the main road into Santa Fe back in the olden days. This was the last stretch before the Spanish and Indians reached the plaza. They rode horses, wagons, and mostly walked thousands of miles through the desert before they got to here. They were really happy once they reached this point."

"No, really, Dad," he came back, just as fast, "*Gears of War* could . . . "

Luckily, we had just passed the intersection where Hickox Street reaches Agua Fría, so I quickly pointed out that just ahead, west of this area, is where rebels cut off the head of the governor of New Mexico in 1837 and used it as a kickball.

"Really?!!!" he replied, finally giving me his undivided attention. "They played kickball with his head?"

I realized right then that the lad was at the point where plain ol' history just wasn't cutting it for him, so I had to make it "sexy" by mixing decapitation and sports—a common maneuver of historians who tell this story to get the attention of uninterested youth and adults alike.

Of course, I was referring to the 1837 Chimayó Rebellion, in which the appointed governor, Albino Pérez, was decapitated by an angry group of rebels. The governor and some of his Mexican military men had already been defeated by another group of rebels near Pojoaque and he was forced to flee back to Santa Fe.

Pérez was newly appointed by the Mexican government and he was extremely disliked by norteños, who immediately considered him an outsider because they were used to one of their own rising through the ranks to become leader. (Sounds as if things haven't changed much, eh?) The locals considered Pérez a carpetbagger of sorts. He liked to gamble and they accused him of using the public treasury to finance his habit rather than for its intended purpose of bolstering the military. Pérez didn't help himself either, because he tried to raise taxes on New Mexicans to replenish government coffers that were mostly depleted by the chicanery and corruption of the officials, including the governor.

Although he left his wife down south in Old Mexico while he was governor up north, the pious local citizenry also despised Pérez because he had fathered an illegitimate child with his house servant just after he settled into his new digs in Santa Fe.

Yes, old Agua Fría Street has many stories to tell, its once dirt path covered by many layers of blacktop, which mostly have been successful in containing the history that the asphalt covers.

Hundreds if not thousands of motorists in a hurry to get from one side of town to the other and then quickly back again probably have no idea that Agua Fría Street once was the end of an arduous northern journey from Mexico City on a series of paths known as El Camino Real and the Chihuahua Trail.

Poor old Gov. Pérez had no idea he would meet his violent fate along this thoroughfare when he first traveled through Agua Fría on his way to become the grand master of the plaza. And many other governors before him met their unfortunate but less violent fate via the Agua Fría way, albeit in the other direction.

You see, back when the Spanish government dictated the dust here, the first order of business among newly installed administrations was to hold a public hearing at which the citizenry and clergy were able to offer testimony against the old administration. More often than not, the outgoing government officials were sent back to Mexico shackled in chains for the atrocities they had committed in office against the citizens and the Indians.

Yep, and that included none other than our own beloved Don Diego de Vargas, who at one time in the early 1700s found himself in chains, probably in the back of a slow-moving carreta and fantasizing about rich silver deposits in the Ortíz Mountains as he began his journey south on the Agua Fría path. Of course, Vargas rebounded as a hero and he returned to New Mexico to serve another term as governor before he died of a feverish illness while he led troops in search of rebellious Indians in the Río Abajo country near what is now Bernalillo.

I'm sure that's something I'll never see in my lifetime—a Don Diego de Vargas in chains atop a carreta float during the Fiesta's Historical/Hysterical Parade. Such a sight just might be too harsh on today's citizens, who also would undoubtedly frown upon the governor's head being used as a kickball. But on the other hand, they just might love to see some of today's outgoing officials in chains on a slow-moving carreta crossing the new Camino Alire bridge on their way to La Cienega and points southward via the Rail Runner tracks.

But nothing that harsh will ever happen here again. Heck, our lawmakers can't even agree to start a discussion on ethics reform, let alone a ball and chain and a comfortable set of furry handcuffs.

Well, I'd already lost my twelve-year-old to the video games. And the next year, when those hormones kicked in and all, I had to work harder to make our history even more sexy for him or to somewhat compete with the cell phone.

I had hoped that Doña Tules in a bikini would have held his attention, at least for a little while.

Pachuco Shoes Pointed the Way

I remember when Nike proudly introduced the new Air Native N7, an athletic sneaker specifically designed for Native Americans. The global company announced that this was the first time it had produced a shoe solely for a specific race or ethnicity. According to a press release, the shoe's design featured several "heritage callouts," including sunrise-to-sunset-to-sunrise patterns on the shoe's tongue and heel. Feather designs adorned the inside and stars on the sole represented the night sky.

At the time I first read about the shoes, which are also devised to be wider and taller at the sole to accommodate the generalized foot traits of Native Americans, I thought it was pretty bold to be identifying physical ethnic traits in our politically correct world. I always thought of Native Americans as light on their feet, not wide on their feet. This work of art, uh, I mean shoe, belonged more in one of the booths down at Indian Market than on the sale rack at Big 5, or so I thought.

But upon further thought, I concluded that I, too, must also be part Native American because I have never really felt comfortable in a pair of regular Nikes either—my feet are also wide, although I never could open my wallet wide enough to buy the top-of-the-line model. That's right. I was too tight to crack for a fancy pair of Air Jordans, so I concluded in my mind that the shoes were too tight as well. Besides, I saw no need for a pair of expensive high-flying basketball sneakers with my three-inch vertical leap. But hey, I made up for my lack of jumping ability by being slow (and with a stealthy hack here and there to the total chagrin of the jughead I was guarding at the time).

But I don't think this is really the first time a shoe company has targeted a specific ethnic group. Poring through all the Hush Puppies, the penny loafers, the Converse Chuck Taylors, the Pro-Keds, the wooden shoes of Holland, or even OJ's Dingo boots, I could have sworn that somewhere in my youth there was a shoe specifically designed for Chicanos.

It's all becoming so clear now. The footwear of my knee-high days was enough to strike fear into any normal breathing lad walking home from baseball practice. Yep, I'm talking about the feared pachuco shoes. Now if there was ever a shoe designed for Chicanos, it was the pachuco shoe, that sleek black-leather model that ran high on the ankles and careened down to a single pointy tip at the toes. In tamer parts of the world these distinct shoes were also known as Beatle Boots.

Now we didn't always call them pachuco shoes. They were also known as "fence climbers" because those pointed toes fit perfectly into the diamond openings of a chain link fence. Fence climbers were especially handy when you were being chased by the cops, or maybe an angry merchant, or more than likely a group of well-meaning (or shall I say, well, mean) fellas who were also wearing pachuco shoes.

But as I've said before, it seems that as the real estate values skyrocketed in our fair city, the demand for pachuco shoes waned exponentially. I haven't seen any around in quite a while, either on the shoe racks at Walmart or on the feet of any of those aging *vatos* I once feared down at the municipal baseball fields—that's Salvador Pérez to most of you citizens different and the train park to all of you Red Sox fans from Back East. I am not ashamed to admit that I still have PTSD from the old days: Pachuco Traumatic Stress Disorder!

Now if there were still any pachucos around, I bet Nike could sell quite a few pairs of shoes designed for them as well. Maybe they could call them the "Air Chuke, O.C.," perfect for those times when you'd rather hop the fence than go all the way around the ball field to the ticket gate. They could also put a little tread on the bottoms so that they wouldn't be so slippery, like the ones back in my day.

Come to think of it, I recall that the pachuco shoes also ran narrow, so there was no way my wide ol' Shrek hoof could fit in one anyway. I had to climb fences the old-fashioned way, in my clunky Chuck Taylors with an occasional rip of my jeans in the process. And by the way, in case you're wondering, the pachucos usually caught me well before I got to the fence. My lack of jumping ability usually resulted in my getting jumped.

I guess I'm really glad deep inside that pachuco shoes went by the wayside. Now all I have to worry about are them young fellas who wear their pants halfway down their *como se llamas*. I think that if one of those tough guys tried to climb a fence in a hurry, he'd rip them stylish trousers right down the middle. You know, it's really quite the challenge to run, jump, and climb with a giddyup like Gumby.

For as long as I can remember, my elders always told me not to get caught with my pants down. I wonder if, when these low-trouser-wearing fashionistas are my age, they'll tell their own blood rebels to "not get caught with their pants up."

Who'd have thunk that the plumber's butt-crack look would be in vogue for everyone in public to see, and not just the distressed housewife with a clogged kitchen sink. But at least these young fellas have the decency to wear some normal-hanging, colorfully patterned boxers underneath and they're passing on the eventually transparent white briefs of our youth.

If they didn't, then there'd be a lot more imaginative places to park your bike. Either that or there'd be a lot more targets to direct a laser-focused pachuco shoe besides scaling a fence or scaring a Little Leaguer in his uniform walking home after the game.

Balloons That Go Burst in the Night

It was always so special when I looked into the excited eyes of my youngest son when he talked about Santa Claus. He was still at that single-digit age when he wholeheartedly believed that Santa landed his sleigh on the roof and came down the chimney with all the presents the tyke had been wishing for ever since his bony, bloody, leaky Scream Halloween costume was finally packed back into the box.

On the other hand, there was my other boy. Yeah, the other one who just turned teenager going on any age older than that. The one who proudly boasted that if you heard something on the roof late on Christmas Eve, it might be a good idea to call the cops.

I think the older boy wholeheartedly believed in the white-bearded fella just a year before. I guess it was around the Fourth of July, just before he turned teenager, by the way, when he fessed up that his older cousin had read him that *National Enquirer* story we all eventually hear about Santa Claus. You know, "Santa Claus Exposed" or "Santa Enters Home, Takes instead of Gives" or "Maw Claims It Was Santa Claus until Paw Saw Bill."

My teenaged lad boasted that he knew the tabloid version when we threatened him that Santa wouldn't visit him if he kept up the tomfoolery. Lucky for us, the little one was down by the river throwing rocks when his older brother proudly announced his summertime Christmas revelation.

So after that, we had to practice a quasi–Casey Stengel style of parenting with the two. Some of you might remember Stengel as that flamboyant baseball manager who once said, "The secret of managing is to keep the guys who hate you away from the guys who are undecided."

Only we tried a somewhat looser variation of this Stengel logic with the magic of Santa Claus, among other things. You know, like not letting the debate get started between the one who believes in Kris Kringle and the one who proclaims he knows about Kris Kringle.

It's a mighty fine line, believing vs. knowing, that usually gets erased by older cousins or siblings, or maybe by someone in the schoolyard with older cousins or siblings who couldn't wait to ambush some other blissful child on one of those fateful days in December.

But you gotta believe in something, as they used to say in Little League, and I don't think you can ever stop being a kid as long as you hold fast to something magical. It's always such a heartbreaker when you reach an epiphany that totally dispels what you truly believed before.

Like the day I watched a documentary on TV about the construction of Hoover Dam, that good ol' concrete wonder, where, in about a five-minute drive, it's a whole hour's difference from one side (Nevada) to the other (Arizona) during Daylight Saving Time. I was always led to believe, and it just might have been by a tour guide at the dam itself, that during the construction of Hoover there were many men who were buried alive after they accidentally fell into the wet concrete as it was being poured.

Later, this sharp-talking fella comes on the documentary and lightheartedly mentions that the stories about construction workers getting buried alive are just myths. The Hoover spokesman on the film said that workers poured the concrete only two or three feet at a time and it would be pretty near impossible to not be able to save anyone who accidentally fell in. He also said that sometimes workers would put boots upside down in the wet cement to make it look like someone went down head first and that's probably how all that dam lore got started.

But the hissing sound heard in my living room that night from my balloon getting burst wasn't all that loud because there was another revelation just a few years before that had already let some air out of it. That's when another belief of mine was smashed like a plump water balloon hitting the pavement. Yep, there was a loud hissing noise coming out of my balloon when I read that a local historian said she had proof that the Miraculous Staircase at the Loretto Chapel downtown was, indeed, built by a skilled Frenchman who also worked on the Basilica St. Francis Cathedral in the nineteenth century.

A saintly, mysterious carpenter named Joseph who only had a saw and wooden mallet didn't build our fantastic staircase after all. Whoever cooked up that story about Joseph had that centuries-old, oft-repeated story tossed out by another cook like week-old Thanksgiving turkey.

But hey, this is Santa Fe and there are lot more neighborly stories around and some of them are doozies. I guess our childhood balloons inevitably burst the older and more knowledgeable we get and we eventually end up with fewer balloons at the end of our lives. That's why it's so refreshing to see a youngster get excited about Santa Claus, or the Easter bunny, or the tooth fairy, or that long-lost rich uncle who might make it possible to buy a house in Santa Fe.

Heck, let's throw La Llorona in there too, for the adults, along with leprechauns, winning the lottery, and weapons of mass destruction. Like those legendary coaches said, "ya gotta believe," at least until you hear the hissing sound.

It used to be fun waiting with my little one for Santa Claus to come sliding down the chimney. He always waited for a package that hopefully came from Best Buy at the North Pole. And I always waited with him for a box of new balloons.

Code Talkers Throw Them Off

Back in my newspaper reporting days, the police scanner was my constant companion, sort of like today's cell phone. There usually wasn't a moment during the workweek when I wasn't listening to the constant chatter of the city police officers, county sheriff's deputies, or fire-department dispatchers keeping in communication with each other and the pulse of the city.

I admit that I was somewhat of an ambulance chaser at the time, and it was my job to listen to the scanner to follow the action wherever it was taking place. The good folks at the *Journal North* even gave me my own scanner to plug in at my house and later a hand-held portable that I could essentially take anywhere—into church, on a fishing trip, to the movies, or even on a date.

When a dispatcher announced over the scanner that a crime had taken place or a fire was fully engaged, the next thing I had to do was pay close attention for the location. That's right. Police reporters do have some buzzwords in common with real estate agents—location, location, location.

In police talk, or code if you will, that's called the 10-20, or just plain 20 for short. So if someone ever asks you on your cell phone, "Hey, man, what's your 20?" you'll know they're asking for your whereabouts in police code.

And be sure not to confuse 10-20 with 4/20. A few years ago, a youngster, in his twenties, informed me that 4/20 is also a code and a date that youngsters used to signal each other to call in sick, ditch school, or otherwise be at some other 10-20 than where they were supposed to be. Then they'd hit an alternate 10-20 and proceed to 4/20, or in other words (or numbers), fill the peace pipe with wacky tobacky and hit it until 4/21.

Now in the spontaneous world of police scanners, it helped me tremendously to be a local bloke—a santefesino, Santa Fe Demon, *puro* Vigilbilly. There are just some paths through the city that a local driver knows where to steer—how to go as the crow flies, how to get into the wind, how to beat the madding crowd. First rule, don't go St. Francis Drive!

But usually a regular Joe uses such shortcuts to get away from the cops, not to follow them. Sometimes I would jump in my car and race to a crime scene so fast that I would beat the cops there, or the ambulance or the fire truck. There's no better feeling that a police reporter gets than when he's able to talk to a witness before a policeman (or a lawyer, for that matter), who usually tells him not to talk to a reporter. Oops! Of course, just like any policeman or fireman will tell you, you never really know what you're going to encounter when you pull up to a situation. One of the first things I learned on this, my first professional job fresh out of college, is that you don't go jumping into your car every time a dispatcher announces a 10-20 over the airwaves.

Police have other codes also, and you learn to train your ears to pay attention to the big ones, mainly Code 1, which means homicide, Code 2, which stands for rape, and Code 3, meaning robbery.

Yep, 1-2-3—these codes were the big three! As I've written before, I had just come to this job fresh out of college where I had studied another big three—reading, writing, and 'rithmetic. Then this wide-eyed college boy (because that's who hardened newspaper editors usually throw in there to cover the cops because nobody else wants to) had a crash course in the other three R's of the real world: rape, robbery, and rigor mortis.

I quickly realized codes and numbers come at you fast and furious in the police and fire world, as do acronyms like POA, PD, FD, BPOE, FOP, FOE, and hut, hut, hut—oh wait, that's football. Then all these uniformed types unwind at each other's houses and their code becomes BYOB.

One time, I rushed to a possible crime scene when I definitely heard on the scanner "Possible Code 1, 10-20 at . . ." Of course, I jumped into my car and rushed over to a crime scene where a woman had been found dead in her condominium and it appeared she'd been there for more than a week. I didn't get there before the cops because sometimes police use different code words or numbers for their usual codes to throw off curious reporters who tend to get in the way at crime scenes and talk to people who have pertinent information. Other times, a reporter will miss scanner calls as they are happening because he might be at some private 10-20 seeing a man about a horse.

As I waited around in the parking lot in front of the woman's home for one of the cops to make a statement about the situation, I kept a lookout for reporters from other local newspapers or TV stations, hoping they wouldn't show up. In our own code, we called the other reporters "brand X," and we used alternate code in our own monitored two-way radio communications to throw them off, a technique we learned from the cops. We'd say stuff like "Meet you at the 10-20 at 4:20 in about twenty—and don't forget about that 20 you owe me!" When it comes to rivalries among newspapers and other outlets, reporters are just like the customers at the local ice cream shop—they want the scoop, the tastier the better and before everybody else.

So, finally, a police captain comes out of the deceased woman's house and announces that the situation is not a suspicious Code 1 after all, but rather an unattended death—Code "I forgot the number." He said she died from the DTs.

Hmmm, DTs? I didn't really know what he meant, but I played along and I quoted him directly, just passing along the information like a good tape recorder. For years, I thought the DTs meant "detoxification" and it was only recently that a really smart lady corrected me and pointed out that the DTs actually stood for delirium tremens, also known as "the horrors," "the shakes," "rum fits," or "jitterbugs," among other things describing excruciating withdrawal from alcohol and drugs.

A chill went up my spine because I thought these were the same symptoms people get when they read my writing. So if you ever have to go to a secret 10-20 on 4/20 to read this column, just say you're going "Code DT." Well, maybe not, because Code DT could also stand for a MAGA rally. YIKES!!!

This Used to Be a Free Country

Every once in a while, someone will ask me the exact location of my favorite private place in Santa Fe or even the whole of the state of New Mexico.

Now, back in my whippersnapper days, I would usually tell them the honest-to-goodness soothing location where I wanted to go to get away from the malarkey and shenanigans and pressure of it all. Sometimes, it seemed, the questioners listened, and sometimes they didn't.

It wasn't until after some of these favorite spots became completely overgrown with other solitude seekers that I began to realize that my big mouth might have had something to do with a particular location's newfound popularity. Either that or I would return to my *resolana* and there would be a sign announcing a new housing development or maybe a new fence with a No Trespassing sign. Or maybe it was just a big, deep, work-for-hire backhoe trench that prevented any vehicles from passing through the well-worn road because so many other people began going there and the sheer numbers of bottle/can throwers, or diaper/mattress chuckers, or insulation/concrete unloaders ruined it for the rest of us.

It's sort of like that famous Yogi Berra line about a restaurant he used to frequent in New York: "Nobody goes there anymore. It's too popular."

I think if you talk to any random local, they'll pretty much tell you the same thing. It used to be that you just had to go out to the Buckman motocross racetrack right off the then dirt Buckman Road to get away from it all. And now, lo and behold, the four-lane NM 599 Veterans Highway took a beeline path right through the gut of that once special serene spot where countless underage kegger parties occurred over the decades.

Or how about Hyde Memorial State Park? For years we thought nothing of throwing a couple of sleeping bags in the car and just pulling up nearly anywhere up there and getting some rest for the night—or any time of day or year for that matter. I wish I could have filmed the face of any random Santa Fe local the first time he was confronted by a park ranger who informed him that from then on he had to pay to hang out there.

"What, five bucks?!!!" the usual reply. "I've been coming up here all my life. We never had to pay before!"

And of course at some time or another, repeat that same Pay to Enter scenario at the entrance to the old dump, camping at Jack's Creek in Pecos, parking on a downtown street or at an event on the rodeo grounds, entering the Fort Marcy Complex or your kid's grade-school basketball game or the burning of Zozobra—or even the bar at El Farol.

Or, just for laughs, commuting that one morning many years ago when the late Pojoaque Pueblo governor Jake Viarrial decided to blockade US 84/285 and charge each vehicle a toll fee. That is, until a couple of fighter jets flew by and let off a couple of sonic booms, or so the legend goes, and he quickly backed off. And no, that wasn't the reason they named a nearby Pojoaque laundromat "Jake's Dirty Shorts."

Oh well, at least ol' Jake provided everyone involved with an honest excuse, for a change, for being late to work in Santa Fe.

A couple of my college buddies from San Felipe Pueblo once admitted to me during an interestingly revealing "two-kegger" moment that sometimes, when they needed money to go into Albuquerque, they would randomly stop nonresident cars heading into the pueblo. Then they'd charge the occupants an entrance fee until they each had enough money to go into Burque to take in a burger, a pop, and a show. Man, talk about an indigenous renewable resource!

Just like the last time a group of us backpackers had to stop our truck on a forest road leading to the wilderness trailhead to hear one local fella tell us that we needed to pay a toll to pass through the land grant, for upkeep of the road and all, you know. Well, we didn't have any money because we were going somewhere you didn't need it. However, we did have plenty of dehydrated dinners, hot dogs, rope, matches, dog food, and liquid painkillers, so he settled for a couple of our Bud Lights instead.

Yep, even if somebody asked me today the exact location of my favorite place to go, I'd have to give them some Yogi Berra–type line like "I don't go there no more. It costs two bits and, as we all know, a dollar ain't worth as much as it used to." (Of course, for all you out there who know me, I'll naturally attribute that line to Yogi Barela.)

I guess it's just a fact of life today that most anywhere we go, we expect a charge or fee or more than likely a fine if we refuse to pay. Whoever coined that old saying "The best things in life are free" obviously never had to find a parking spot near the plaza to hit Spanish Market, Indian Market, or the Children's Pet Parade, events that are all still free to attend by the way.

I once knew this guy who used the old circular pull top off old Coke cans to fool the parking meters downtown into thinking it was a dime. Well, the city eventually got wise and invested in new meters and, instead of the city coffers, the old detachable Coke tops ended up at the landfill, on the street next to the parking meters, or on the ground at some of my favorite out-of-the-way places.

I remember this one guy on the radio asked me where my favorite spot was and I wish I had said, "Your house! What's that address again?" Instead, I told him, in my finest diplomatic form, that there were just too many nice places in this beautiful country to narrow it down to only one.

Of course, my imaginary friend Yogi Barela tells us, "Our beloved City Different is no longer Santa Free. It's Santa Fee."

New Mexicans Really Love Their Sports

It never fails. Whenever I go over to a friend's house for some type of celebration or another, I end up in front of the television with my kids watching a football game, or basketball, or baseball, or anything but golf, bowling, and, God forbid, poker.

On one occasion, the kids really weren't watching a game—they were too busy turning into jelly brains with their PlayStation controllers in hand and not a clue about what was going on around them. Then I walked in the room, pulled rank like the bully I am, and made them change the channel so that I could take my turn at being a zombie in front of the television—and become just as oblivious to the "mature" chitchat reverberating around me in the process. (Gee, and I often wonder where those couch-potato kids get those jelly-brained habits.)

That abrupt channel change must have broken the party ice because, before you know it, some more "mature" stragglers came in to watch the Eagles whale on the Cowboys, one of the favorite teams of my friend's daughter-in-law, who also wandered in.

That's right, this young newlywed sat down and starting batting out statistics, players' names, team names, and just about anything else that is basically learned when you religiously watch ESPN, FOX Sports, or CNN on TV every night. Curiously, though, she didn't have cable at her home back in Texas.

Rather, she gleaned her knowledge of professional sports the old-fashioned way—from a lifelong love of organized athletics, the newspaper, and gatherings around the water cooler. Oh yeah, and she and her new husband were doing pretty well playing fantasy football on the Internet, where she picked up her superior knowledge of that current football season's statistical details.

After I finally admitted that my favorite team was the perennially bottom dwelling Oakland Raiders, she looked startled that I even had a team. Then she revealed that her new husband, my friend's son, didn't really follow sports when she met him. She said that one time he matter-of-factly told her that people from New Mexico weren't into sports at all, probably to cover for her zealous interest in professional sports and his lack thereof.

I guess she really believed him because she genuinely looked surprised when she learned many of us New Mexicans do, indeed, follow professional sports, including my kids, whom I have painstakingly brainwashed since they were infants into liking my favorite teams.

Now knowing my friend's son since he was a wee book-reading lad himself, I knew he was pulling her leg about this general disinterest in sports and all. So I decided to have a little fun as well.

"Yes," I told her, "we do love sports here in New Mexico. In fact there are whole communities that get behind certain teams."

"Really?" she replied, ready to fall hook, line, and sinker. "What do you mean?"

"Well, down south we have this community called Hatch and they call themselves the 'Chile Capital of the World,'" I said. "And do you know what team this community of chile growers roots for?"

"No," she said. "Which one?"

"Why the Miami Heat, of course, because they like it nice and hot down there. And their second-favorite team is the Phoenix Suns."

"Really?" she replied. "Are there any others?"

"Sure, down at Truth or Consequences and Elephant Butte they really like the Los Angeles Lakers," I told her in my best poker face. "And if the Lakers are stinking that year, then they'll pull for the New York Islanders or the Florida Marlins or the Seattle Mariners.

"And they really don't care for the Carolina Hurricanes or the San Jose Sharks or the Pittsburgh Pirates."

"Wow!" she said. "And all this time I thought you guys didn't like sports."

"Yeah, we sure do," I said, my mind racing at 100 mph trying to think up some more teams to keep this taffy pulling. "In fact, up north there are some people in some small isolated communities who still believe in brujos and brujas and La Llorona and the paranormal and all.

"These norteños are also very religious, so they always pray for the New Orleans Saints to win on Sundays as well as the San Diego Padres. But, on the other hand, they're also very afraid of the Orlando Magic, the New Jersey Devils, and the Washington Wizards."

"Man, he never told me any of this," she said of her husband. "This is too much."

"Of course, down at the state penitentiary they really like one particular team—the Pittsburgh Steelers," I said with conviction. "But that's only because they think they're stealers, you know, like looters. But, you know, some of the other inmates they keep in protective custody like the Nashville Predators."

"But what about the Texas teams?" she asked. "Doesn't anyone around here like any Texas teams?"

"Oh sure," I answered. "But that kind of gets complicated, you know, like a mysterious beautiful woman who loves the Cleveland Cavaliers but will never allow herself to be tamed by one man.

"There are many Native Americans here who are quite passionate about the Cowboys, believe it or not. On the other hand, I don't know if it would be PC to bring up the subject of the Atlanta Braves, the Cincinnati Reds, the Golden State Warriors, or the Washington Redskins around them.

"And the Cleveland Indians, I won't even go there. But I will mention that there are a bunch of crazy Chicanos up north who love the Cleveland Browns first and then the Minnesota Wild and the Atlanta Thrashers."

"So what you're saying is that whole communities in New Mexico will get behind the one team that they can identify with?" she asked.

"Well not necessarily," I answered. "Sometimes there are little pockets of people who like to be different from the whole.

"For instance, the folks down at The Cuttery like the Los Angeles Clippers, and the fire department dudes like the Calgary Flames.

"But, on the other hand, groundskeepers at the State Capitol detest the Toronto Maple Leafs, and those inside the governor's office on the fourth floor of the capitol could do without the Ottawa Senators. And there's a whole bunch of guys at the spa who really get behind the Green Bay Packers."

By that time, the game on TV had ended, so I told her that in the days before organized city-league sports and television here in Santa Fe, they used to make the kids box for entertainment. But now, the only time that happens is when the little tykes are arguing over who gets the good PlayStation controller.

And if there are no boxing gloves around, then we have to resort to some great old-fashioned professional leg pulling, you know, Chicago Bull style.

More Whining and Less Dining

One time on one of the many call-in contests by KBAC-FM, Radio Free Santa Fe, I won a couple of free tickets to see the Cowboy Junkies at the Lensic Performing Arts Center.

Just before the concert started, a pleasant gentleman from FanMan Productions got up and started talking about future performances in the summer and fall. At one point during his introduction, he enthusiastically blurted out something to the effect of "And we're doing all we can here to save you guys some dough!"

Well, whenever anyone in any position of price-setting says something like that, you can usually see my tight-wadded, freebie-contest-entering, *pinche como se llama* leaping off the milk crate and clapping profusely—and that one Sunday night was no exception.

Except for one thing. There was only a smattering of other people clapping with me and, as I looked around, it seemed like some of the people in the audience looked like they were actually insulted by the remark. In fact, I saw one guy start clapping at first—then he looked around and saw that he was in the applauding minority and he stopped just as quickly before he abashedly slumped in his chair.

Well, after seeing that, I couldn't help but let out one of my famous ear-ringing, lobe-covering vaquero whistles that I only use nowadays when I stick my head out the front door to alert the kids that it's time to come home, or when the Kiwanis guys are taking their sweet time about torching Zozobra. Luckily, they dimmed the lights in the Lensic just after that awkward moment because then nobody could see the face of the loud piker—who seems like he never gets off the rancho much—making all that whistling racket from the free-ticket section.

Of course, that was back in good times, and the economy tanked in the months after and the price of gas and just about everything else went way up. It was also around the time a former US senator from Texas named Phil Gramm remarked that we'd become a "nation of whiners" when it came to the slumping economy. "Let them eat Gramm crackers," I now say of that callous comment from a rich out-of-touch guy who you'll surely never see in the cheap seats applauding anything that helps out struggling Americans.

I wonder, if we fast-forwarded that same scenario and the FanMan man's comment to today, would there be more people in that audience clapping (or whining) today?

Now that we're hearing the word "recession" more often in the news, and everywhere else for that matter, there's been an increase in news stories about cost-saving tips and ways we can stretch the dollar to its breaking point. Some of these tips of late are very useful and some I can remember back to my own childhood days when the word of the week wasn't "Google," it was "frugal."

Yep, sometimes I can see the disappointment in our visitors' eyes when you reveal to them that not everyone in Santa Fe is rich and that, unfortunately, some of us whose families have been here for centuries actually have to move out of town to achieve the American dream of owning a decent home, while earning wages that would achieve at least as much nearly anywhere else in the nation.

But I like to see the excitement come back to their eyes when I tell them of the ways our parents would keep us children amused and the ways we whippersnappers entertained ourselves without having to go to the mall or any other retail outlet to purchase our happiness. For instance, take that state highway between Española and NM 502 that skirts right by Santa Clara Pueblo with stunning views of Black Mesa and the Sangre de Cristo Mountains to the east. Some people now call that road (NM 30) Jim Morrison's Highway.

The late Doors singer remembered it in his memoirs as the location where as a young boy on a family road trip he saw a bunch of "Indians scattered all over the highway, bleeding to death" one early morning in 1947 just after an accident. Morrison wrote that he thought maybe a spirit or two from one of those victims leaped right into his soul. Anyway, right around the time the Doors were in their heyday, in the late 1960s, my dad used to take all of us mocosos in his red Ford Galaxy convertible to that same highway for a Chicano roller coaster ride, not only because it was cheaper, but also because it was a lot closer than driving all the way to Uncle Cliff's in Albuquerque.

You see, back then a pretty sizable section of that two-lane blacktop had a series of good-sized whoop-de-doos. Now for those of you non-motocrossing folks out there, whoop-de-doos are a succession of small hills or bumps on a road or trail that are best enjoyed at a high rate of speed, kind of like riding a motorcycle on the old dirt Buckman Road.

Of course, since we grew up poor, we didn't know those fun humps as whoop-de-doos (the word probably wasn't invented yet). We simply referred to them as the "bumps." Today the bumps have long since been smoothed over as well as the cheap thrills that came along with them. The highway now meets federal safety standards, so there's no possibility of seeing a bunch of little Vigils whoop-de-doing out of an open convertible.

Ask almost any santafesinos older than fifty and they'll surely share some story or another of how they made ends meet while growing up in the olden days of the City Deficient. Things weren't always hunky-dory here in the real estate and development world, but then again there were still plenty of Garcías living on García Street and those living on Cerro Gordo weren't so *gordo* and didn't have to be a fat cat to roost there.

One friend told me that his mom used to wash the cereal boxes so that she would have something to put their Christmas gifts in, usually socks, shorts, and toothbrushes. I can just see the excitement in his eyes after he neatly opened his gift so that his mom could use the wrapping paper next year: "Oh, *chingón*, Santa brought me corn flakes."

Then I would jokingly counter that my mom used to get out one piece of dental floss and then rinse and wipe it each time so that the next sibling could use it. Now being the youngest in the litter, you can see why my teeth ain't so straight and, perhaps, are a little yellow.

Also, promptly turning off lights was a requirement in our house growing up. Today, my kids must think I'm some kind of shrieking shadow because I'm always following them around turning off the lights they turn on, even during the day. And now that the price of electricity has also gone up, I'm starting to think PNM stands for Pay-thru Nose More.

All right, Mr. Gramm, I'm starting to sound a little bit like I'm whining here, but I just hope that I can make it to the point someday where I won't have to clap every time someone announces they're trying to save me some dough. But just as life happens in cycles, I guess penny-pinching is coming back in style again.

(APPLAUSE sign on or off, depending on the checking account balance)

Pigs Are for Chicharrónes

When I was a kid, I always wondered why they chose to have Election Day so close to Halloween. But now that I'm just a little bit older, I know that those events are equally spooky and the fact that they are scheduled so close together might not be a coincidence.

In fact, there are some similar otherworldly days that people celebrate in our neck of the woods between Halloween and Election Day. For instance, the Mexican celebration of el Día de los Muertos, or Day of the Dead, happens the two days after Halloween. So there's always the fringe benefit of not having to rush to put those costumes back in the shed the next morning, that first day of November. Yes, that's when the kids are sneakily chomping down yet more candy for breakfast and many of the rest of us are still suffering through a hangover and too sick to get up and tell the little brats to put the sweets away and eat a more nutritious meal instead, like Sugar Frosted Flakes.

And Día de los Muertos occurs simultaneously with the Roman Catholic holy days of All Saints Day and All Souls Day, which commemorate the known and unknown saints in heaven and those faithfully departed souls who have not yet reached heaven but are waiting their turn in Purgatory—sort of like the anxious political candidates waiting to learn their fate from the electorate (or, perhaps, in the incumbents' case, the jury).

Then, of course, they saved the scariest day (for some of us) of all for last: Election Day. Boy, and that year Barack Obama ran against John McCain and running mate Sarah Palin was a doozy, especially because of all that talk about a pig with lipstick or a pit bull with lipstick or maybe a Rudy Giuliani with lipstick (and a dress). Obama started it all by saying a pig with lipstick is still a pig and he got all the pig lovers up in arms. Then Palin countered with a quip that a pit bull with lipstick is actually a hockey mom.

And photos of ol' Giuliani, who lost in the presidential primary, surfaced of him wearing women's clothing. Some of you might recall the line from that old-favorite holiday song "Rudolph the red-lipped mayor had a very sharp tongue/If you make fun of his high heels, then he won't show you his thong."

But here in politically conscious northern New Mexico, ol' Chicano Confucius likes to advise, "If life throws you pig with lipstick, make chicharrónes." And don't forget to down those tasty little Chicano meatballs with some lemonade made from the lemons that the politicos always seem to throw our way.

Anyway, if you happen to see a pit bull on the street with red lipstick, that's probably not lipstick on his snout at all. It's more than likely blood, which the canine just acquired after he chewed through the chain that was tied to one of the unchecked Siberian elms in the owner's yard. And if you ever happen to see a hockey mom on the street with lipstick, whatever you do, don't ask her, "How much?" Then that lipstick likely will turn into blood really fast—your blood—and you just might end up with a strategically placed hockey stick on your person to boot.

Yep, in that historic election those hopeful political candidates turned good old-fashioned lipstick into lip-schtick and when that got them schtuck, I mean stuck, in the mud, they started to sling that also. Man, and when that lipstick and mud start flying around and splattering all over everything, it not only reminds most of us of a nasty divorce, it makes us long for the days when the only commercials on TV were those for Bud Light, Rolaids, and Pepto-Bismol. Those commercials eventually came back, though, because they're all essentials for before, during, and after Election Day (and Halloween as well).

Back in the old says here in Santa Fe, there were no such things as hockey moms or soccer moms. All we had mostly were *fregazo* moms and gradually they morphed into Little League moms after they built the baseball fields over there at Salvador Perez Park.

Fregazos is one of the nicer local words for fisticuffs or hooks, jabs, uppercuts, and, if there are no churchgoing ladies around, *jodasos* or *chingasos*. Back in the day when there were more pachucos roaming around our now gentrified streets, you naturally saw more fregazo moms down at Safeway, Piggly Wiggly, and Tempo or shopping for lipstick and Band-Aids over at TG&Y and Payless. But just like all of these once famous businesses, the once proud and defiant fregazo moms slowly disappeared from our town as well as the occasional continuation of their jitos' fregazos right there in line while they waited to pay for hydrogen peroxide. And when that happened, it turned into fregazas, or jodasas and chingasas if it wasn't on a Sunday. The fregazo moms have since been replaced by the you-know-whos: You see them to this day getting out of their comfortable SUVs to shop for snack day at Whole Foods, Albertsons, and Smith's, as well as for lipstick and little trophies galore at Target and Walmart.

I'd never thought I'd see the day in America when Election Day actually had the potential to be scarier than Halloween or Día de los Muertos, but it seems to be happening right before our eyes every election cycle. We might be better off if we forgo them all and just celebrate All Saints Day and All Souls Day, because that's what all the politicians pretend to be before an election. It's not until way after that we learn they were better suited for Halloween and Day of the Dead.

But come future elections I think I'm going to vote for the one who promises to rid our streets of pigs with lipstick, pit bulls with lipstick, and all the Siberian elm trees they're chained to as well.

And when this happens, I think it'll be the day when pigs can fly.

José, Can You Sí?

Wow, time sure does fly by when you're having fun, doesn't it? It's been decades since former president Clinton brought worldwide attention to the term "Joe Six-Pack" when he was talking about the dismissal of a lawsuit filed against him by Paula Jones.

If I can recall correctly today, many, many six-packs later (okay, maybe just one or two more "manys"), the former president took some flak from his critics for using the term to describe the average American citizen. He said that as president he had to bridle his true feelings about Jones' allegations, but if he was just Joe Six-Pack, he could have told the world how he really felt.

Now, for all my fellow beer drinkers out there, we know he really would have let his true feelings out, president or not, if he actually drank a six-pack first and then commented to the media. But let's not leave out Hillary, either, because if she also would've drunk a six-pack at the time, I'm sure her true feelings would have let loose as well and ol' Bill would have looked more like Joe Palooka than Joe Six-Pack the next day.

Yep, that Joe Six-Pack crack hit a chord with nearly everybody, but the term can't possibly describe all of the Average Joes out there. I remember thinking at the time that if Clinton really was going to pick a term that accurately pegged the average, true-blue beer drinker, he instead should have said "Joe Twelve-Pack."

And if there were another Regular Joe or two in the room, it probably would've been more accurate to say "Joe Eighteen-Pack" or "Joe Thirty-Pack," especially after a competitive city-league game or something like that. Since we're at it, we might as well throw in a pack of Luckys as well and, after the beer runs out, start callin' in one of those other sweaty fellows, "Joe Shot-o'-Crown."

My, what a difference time makes. Some of the former president's then detractors of the Joe Six-Pack label resurrected the "Joe" label on a much larger scale to serve their own interests. They started using Joe Six-Pack again in their speeches and it's morphed into Joe the Plumber, which they actually used in political commercials.

The actual plumber who caused all this commotion had his life turned upside down in the process and unfortunately was the target of many cracks and the butt of many jokes. All of this and we never saw him inside Josetta the Housewife's kitchen, crouched under the sink looking for his pencil with his pants . . . well, you know. When all this "Joe" hoopla overflowed at the time, I called my own plumber and wanted to get his take on the situation over a six-pack. I'm still waiting for him to show up. I guess some things will never change.

But with all of this rigmarole over Joe Six-Pack and Joe the Plumber, I wonder if Joe the Wine Drinker and Joe the Carpenter are feeling a little left out. And what about all the teetotalers and bored office workers? Are they not average as well?

But ol' Joe Six-Pack and Joe the Plumber aren't alone in the throes of average-dom. Right here in northern New Mexico, the old-timers used to address each other as Joe all the time—right before their real first name. It wasn't uncommon to hear salutations like this, which I have translated for your convenience.

"¡Órale, Joe Ben! Wazzzzzup?"

"Hey, Joe Carlos. What happened yesterday to your *primo*, Joe Henry?"

"He stayed at home all day waiting for the plumber. Now he calls him Joe No-Show."

"How come Leaky Louie didn't show?"

"Joe No-Sé."

"Bummer! Let's go grab a bite at Joe's Diner—your treat!"

"Joe Mama!"

Of course, they didn't always call each other Joe, especially if the other guy was actually named Joe. That would be too confusing, just like if you asked someone if they knew "Joe." In fact, that sort of thing still happens today.

"Hey, you know Joe?"

"Which one?"

"You know . . . JOE!"

"Maybe if I saw him."

I say we need more national political candidates to come over here to New Mexico and pander to some of our own Regular Joes. I'm sure we have a Joe the Plumber of our own under a house somewhere and Lord knows there are Joe Six-Packs all over the place. Heck, there used to be a Joe's Ringside in Las Vegas and many a Joe Palooka came a'staggerin' outta there.

Maybe they could go downtown and point toward the Cathedral and profess their adoration for Joe Quasimodo, no matter how much trouble he stirs up. And that beauty of a woman who's the apple of his eye is a sure bet for some commoner votes as well.

Then they could go to Java Joe's or Cuppa-Joe, where they could share some Joe and discuss what they should call José to appeal to the Hispanic vote. Because there's nothing like some Joe to keep you regular, especially if it's black. But I'm sure they'll pass on the José angle because they really won't know if he's eligible to vote or not.

Well, that presidential election is now well over and all the Joes of the world had their days in the sun, particularly Joe the Plumber, who went back to those darn leaky pipes that awaited him while he shined in front of the cameras. Word has it that he's no longer a plumber and now he's just Forgotten Joe.

And Joe Six-Pack won't be basking in the limelight anymore either. Just as Cinderella's carriage turned back into a pumpkin at midnight, the day after that particular Election Day, all the Joe Six-Packs of the world turned back into the plain ol' *borrachos* everyone thought they were before all the politics.

I guess it's fair to say Joe's days were numbered.

Scary Lessons in Life

It's really a nice feeling now that the blood sugar levels are finally getting back to normal. Halloween's over and most of the kids' hearty stash of candy freeloaded from the neighbors is slowly starting to dwindle.

Having that bowl of sweets staring you in the eye every time you pass by it is a lesson in self-control—whether to grab four (or six) of the little morsels and then asking ten minutes later if you really should come back for more. Aw, why not?

And now that election time is also over, it's going to be nice to finally get the blood-pressure levels back to normal, or as close to normal as possible, especially coupled with all the candy disappearing from the bowl and heading straight for the gut (and your heart). In the days after Halloween, there are also other lessons in self-control—whether or not to believe all the baits of fear offered up by the political candidates in thirty-second or one-minute sound bites. It's always a great relief to be relieved of the candy bites and the sound bites at about the same time!

Conjured-up fear has become so much a part of our daily lives during election cycles lately that it's no wonder the candy disappears from the bowl as fast as it does. Anxiety and bite-sized candy go hand in hand, just as do sweet-caused headaches and Tylenol.

And speaking of fear, I overheard a couple of people talking the other day about what they perceived as the poor quality of education in Santa Fe as well as in New Mexico in general. There seemed to be a tinge of unfounded and conjured-up fear in their conversation when the subject shifted to the public schools in our fair city. Gauging from their tone, sending their children to our public schools would never enter the equation in either of their households. It was obvious that they never went to school here and they really didn't know anyone personally who had children going to public schools here.

I know many hard-working teachers and principals in this town, some of whom I went to school with and others who actually taught me and are still working in the system. These are a dedicated bunch and, if teaching and administering was all they had to do once they arrived at school every morning, then I'm sure more of our schools would be in line with the hunky-dory world expected by the two people I overheard talking.

Recently, a middle-school teacher I know emphasized to me, "You know, if we could pick and choose our students the way private schools do, then we would also have high test scores, high graduation rates, and more students who go on to college. But when there's a problem kid, we have to deal with it. We can't just kick him out of school as the first alternative and then go on our merry way."

I remember several years back when a high-ranking state official in former governor Gary Johnson's administration made a general comment about public school teachers complaining about low pay. In effect, he said that they should "stop the bitching and start teaching." Man, I wish this guy's boss would have ordered him to take over a high school classroom for a month—at a teacher's salary, no less—and then asked him if he felt the same way after his experience.

After his brief stint with a bunch of cantankerous soon-to-be-adults—and they're that way in private schools too, I'll speculate—I'm sure the first thing on his agenda would have been to lobby heavily for the return of corporal punishment, which was pretty much the norm when I was in school. His new mantra probably would have become "Stop the bitching and start the paddling."

But the ironic thing about this situation was that his boss, the outspoken millionaire governor, chose to send his own children to our public schools and I never once heard him complain publicly about the quality of education they were receiving. There was no fear of the public schools on his part even though, again ironically, he championed the cause of public-funded vouchers to help families pay for students to attend private schools.

When my son was younger, I used a form of sound-bite fear to jolt him back into line if I noticed his grades at his public school were slipping: "You better start getting your act together at school or I'm going to send you to Prep." Usually, he would fearfully reply, "No, no. I'll start doing better!"

The other day I again tried using that fear-mongering sound bite on the teenager and the oats-feeling middle schooler fearlessly responded, "Yeah right. You can't afford to send me to Prep!"

What could I say? He put me right back in my place: Casa de Pobre. Yes, grasshopper, he's learning how to debate and rebut well in public school. But if ever I can afford it, he's no longer going to Prep. Nope, I'm sending his little smarty-pants *como se llama* to the New Mexico Military Institute. He's becoming way too much like me.

Sometimes when people asked me where he went to school, I often saw the look of puzzlement in their eyes when I told them that I still had solid confidence in our public schools. Then I had a little fun with my own fifteen-second sound bite at the expense of their fears.

"Oh yeah," I'd reply to them. "I love that (public) school. He's getting a solid education in *cholo*-nomics, *macho*-matics, *ruca*-history, nunya-business, and don't forget *pachu*-cology. And let's not forget the concise geography lessons they learn on the playground: Southside, Eastside, Westside, and, maybe, a little Northside between applied-intoxicology.

"And after school he's a member of the Grass Club. Sometimes, since I'm a writer, they even ask me to go down to the yearbook class and teach Chicano-lism."

Yep, my little insider misinformation about our public schools is just about as absurd as the barrage of fear-mongering sound bites we have to endure before the election. But even though it just might leave a bad taste in the mouth, it's nothing that can't be remedied by some of those sweet leftover Halloween bites.

Oh yeah, and maybe just a little bite of parental involvement too.

Getting to Know Each Other Better

Many years ago while I was sharing a few beers with a good buddy, the jovial mood suddenly became serious and this usually pretty funny guy turned to me and announced, "Arnold, if you really want to know me, go see these three movies—*The Godfather Part II*, *The Deer Hunter*, and *Taxi Driver*."

Well, what could I say? This guy had just shared part of his soul with me, so I felt obliged to return the gesture. "Okay, if you really want to know me," I replied in earnest, trying my best to keep a straight face, "go see these three movies—*Animal House*, *The Blues Brothers*, and *The Nutty Professor*."

Yep, there we were after a hard day's work on a construction site, a wannabe Robert DeNiro and John Belushi each trying to do his best santafesino Marlon Brando imitations—"You don't understand. I coulda had class. I coulda been a finisha. I coulda been somebody. Instead of a laborer, which is what I am. Let's face it!"

Of course, this all happened before there were VCRs or DVD players and I didn't think to ask him if it still counted if I didn't actually go experience his heartfelt movies on the big screen at the Lensic, the Coronado Twins, El Paseo, or even the Yucca Drive-In. Would I really know him if I didn't actually "go see" these flicks but rather rented and watched them on a VCR in the comfort of my own living room without the luxury of $6 popcorn, $5 candy, and a newborn baby spiritedly developing his lungs in the seat right in front of me?

Some years later I made the mistake of relating this story to a bunch of my softball cronies while we were crying in our beers after losing a close game to some hated rivals. "Arnold," one of them said to me, apparently speaking for the rest of those snickering jugheads, "if we really wanted to know you, we'd go see *Big Top Pee-Wee, Slam Dunk Ernest,* and *Forrest Gump.*"

Man, those movies were fighting words. I couldn't let these clowns pick out the motion pictures that define me. "Oh yeah?" I barked back, not backing down an inch. "If you guys really want to know me, go see these three movies—*Rambo: First Blood, Braveheart,* and *The John Holmes Story.*" All right, I admit that's a stretch, but the movies we think describe ourselves usually aren't the flicks that others see in us, and we tend to exaggerate when it comes to ourselves as well as others. But I wasn't about to let those boneheads off the hook.

"And if I want to know you guys," I continued, "I'll go see these movies—*12 Angry Men, The Dirty Dozen, 12 Monkeys, Eight Men Out,* and *The Birdcage.* Oh yeah, and any of the *Jackass* movies!" WHAP! I sure showed them.

Well, by that time the banter was out of control, not to mention the quality of the insults. We descended from classy movies down to television series (think *Gilligan's Island, Get Smart,* and *The Flying Nun*), down to songs we hear on the radio (as in, "Bad to the Bone," "I'm a Sex Machine," and, when talking about them, "I Feel Pretty"), and then on to breakfast cereals. "Oh yeah, if I want to know you, I'll eat these three cereals—nuts and flakes, puffed wheat, and Fruity Pebbles!"

There's no doubt that most of us can identify with the movies that somehow reflect certain times of our lives. Way back when, in my single college days, my first serious relationship with a woman was somewhat tumultuous. I guess it can best be summed up by someone going to see these three productions—*Fatal Attraction, The War of the Roses,* and *Misery.* Do I even dare mention *Psycho, Single White Female,* and *The Nutcracker?*

Today, I can't help but feel my cache of self-identifying films has become dated, especially when my kids are coming home from the video store with titles like *Knocked Up*, any *Jackass* movie, and *Dude, Where's My Car?* I thank the Lord that somehow I've matured and moved on to other more pleasant movies like *Driving Miss Daisy*, *It's a Wonderful Life*, and *Viva Las Vegas*.

But for those of us with kids, especially teenagers who suddenly bring home new mysterious friends, there are some movies that we can tell our childless friends to go see that will help them understand our current parenting predicament—movies such as *Problem Child*, *The Warriors*, and *A Clockwork Orange*. Don't even think of getting me started on the movies I'd send them to see regarding their friends, like *The Bad Seed*, *Village of the Damned*, and *The Omen*. It's hard enough just letting them go to the video store by themselves.

There I go exaggerating again, but it's so easy with such a large database of films to pick from. There are even movies that can describe our politicians or, perhaps, a long turnover of public school superintendents we've had to endure. For instance, go see *The Out-of-Towners*, *Gone in 60 Seconds*, *The Carpetbaggers*, and, of course, *Harry in Your Pocket* and *Dirty Rotten Scoundrels*.

There are even movies for our beloved Realtors as well, such as *Man in the Middle*, *Other People's Money*, *Easy Money*, and, naturally, *For a Few Dollars More*. Obviously, because the price of a home in Santa Fe has skyrocketed out of reach for most regular folk due to the speculation and all, a feel-good good movie to see about real estate agents here is *Hang 'Em High*.

And for all you single guys, there might be a warning flag if your new sweetie comes home from the grocery store with scissors, duct tape, bleach, and *Thelma and Louise*, *Monster*, and *Sybil*. But she's a keeper if she comes home with beer, chips, pizza, and *Gladiator*, *10*, and *Everything You Wanted to Know About Sex* But Were Afraid to Ask*.

And ladies, if he comes home with wine, cheese, napkins, and *La Cage Aux Folles*; *Zorro, the Gay Blade*; and *Brokeback Mountain*, I think *Friends* is all you are going to be. But at least that's better than if he comes home with scissors, duct tape, bleach, and *Anger Management*, *Once Were Warriors*, and *The Boston Strangler*.

Well, my friends, I don't think I'm going to have enough time on my hands to keep going to the movies so that I can get to know all of you. I think reality is much more bizarre than fiction.

Just ask my very good friend over there, *Harvey*.

Acknowledgments

I recognize my departed dad, Benito, and late mother, Margaret, both of whose love, stories, and personal experiences and insights helped a wee lad like me—who listened some of the time—develop an appreciation for an old New Mexican world that, unbeknownst to us all, was fleeting by the second. My late brother and best friend, Gerry, must also be mentioned. Had his life not been tragically taken by an unknown hit-and-run driver in 1969 while he was happily riding his bicycle just hours after school let out for the summer, I would not have developed at an early age an appreciation for life and those around me and the many colorful stories they have to offer.

I also acknowledge Larry Calloway for dropping my name to *Journal North* editor Mark Oswald, who first took a chance, then allowed me to continue with "¡Órale! Santa Fe" for nearly five years; and to Anna Gallegos and Lisa Pacheco at the Museum of New Mexico Press for approving a shelf life for much longer. I also appreciate the encouragement and feedback from many of the column's readers who emailed me, unexpectedly dropped into my office to meet me, or stopped me on the street to offer me greetings, compliments, and encouragement, oftentimes during periods of uncertainty as to where the next column would come from. Especially, I am grateful to my Aunt Angie, the last remaining sibling of my mom's five sisters and one brother, who often encouraged me to keep writing and reminded me that my mother would have enjoyed my columns (she passed away a couple of years before they began).

My sister Diana always says, especially after funeral eulogies, that it's best to not start mentioning names because someone will always be left out and there will be hurt feelings. Therefore, I resist the temptation to name all the rest of my family, my excellent teachers and professors throughout the years, my athletic coaches, my professional mentors, all my former coworkers, and all my friends who unknowingly provided much chiste to this project. All of you have influenced me for the better in one way or another, and I hope that somewhere herein you will recognize where that happened!

About the Author

Arnold Vigil was born in Santa Fe, was raised in northern New Mexico, and graduated from Santa Fe High School. Vigil earned a bachelor's degree in journalism/English and political science from New Mexico Highlands University (NMHU), where he was a reporter and then editor of the student newspaper, *La Mecha*, and later a photographer with the university's public information office.

While in high school and college, Vigil also worked as a gas station attendant, forest firefighter, construction worker, dishwasher, movie projectionist, lifeguard, boxing coach, and busboy. During college he worked for a year and half through a cooperative education program at the Los Alamos National Laboratory employees' newspaper, the *Los Alamos NewsBulletin*, where he mentored under working professionals in writing, photography, and technical editing.

Shortly after graduating from NMHU, Vigil was hired as a police and courts reporter for the *Albuquerque Journal*'s northern bureau, *Journal North*, which was in fierce competition with the city's local newspaper, the *Santa Fe New Mexican*.

After a handful of years of chasing cops, lawyers, and ambulances, Vigil became an editor at *New Mexico Magazine*, where he wrote feature articles, edited numerous books and nearly a decade's worth of the state's official vacation guide, developed product lines for resale, helped establish and maintain the website, and provided supplemental photography for all of the above.

Some of the many books Vigil edited and produced there include *Forever New Mexico*; *Enduring Cowboys: Life in the New Mexico Saddle*; *Backtracks: Time Travels through New Mexico*; *The Allure of Turquoise*; *Retirement New Mexico*; and *Santa Fe, The Chief Way*. Vigil also wrote "¡Órale! Santa Fe," a bi-monthly column for *Journal North* from 2004 to 2008.

When his career at the magazine ended in 2011, Vigil worked as a senior archivist in the Historical Division of the New Mexico State

Archives and Records Center before retiring from state government three years later. He says he was like "a kid in a candy store" during his time at the archives, surrounded by all of the fascinating historical documents and like-minded history lovers. Vigil also worked for the New Mexico State Senate Majority Office as a public relations officer and for one session as a security guard during legislative sessions from 2012 to 2019.

He is currently restoring his family's historical home and irrigated property north of Santa Fe while writing freelance for the *Santa Fe New Mexican, Journal North, Taos News*'s *Land Water People Time*, and other assorted advertorial projects. He also worked as a movie and television extra in productions such as *Blood Father; Cliffs of Freedom; Better Call Saul*; and *Midnight, Texas*.

Vigil feels fortunate that he was born in time to experience life during the waning years of authentic, old-time Santa Fe before the historic city began to dramatically change while he was a teenager in the late 1970s. These changes, he observes, not only made Santa Fe more internationally renowned but also signaled less of that downhome feeling amongst its citizens, with growing divides between locals and newcomers on many fronts—cultural, economic, educational, political, and historical.